"Not all that far into *Connected towar[d]* [...] offer a prayer of thanksgiving for this extr[...] blessedly devoid of thick theological or church jargon, Daniella Zsupan-Jerome shows how digital culture supports rather than undermines our human longing for connection. Her clear and thorough analysis of key documents reveals the Vatican's longstanding commitment to a theology of communications anchored in Christ and transcending particular forms of time- and technology-bound media. I believe *Connected toward Communion* should be required reading for all ministers and church leaders across and beyond denominational boundaries."

> —Meredith Gould, PhD
> Author of *The Social Media Gospel: Sharing the Good News in New Ways*

"Professor Zsupan-Jerome does an admirable job in bringing the church's theology of communication and teaching on communication, largely developed for an era of mass media, to bear on the world of social media. She offers a great resource for those who wish to reflect theologically on communication. *Connected toward Communion* will prove invaluable for students, for media professionals in the church, and for anyone engaging in online religion."

> —Paul A. Soukup, SJ
> Professor and Department Head
> Communication Department
> Santa Clara University

"With this gem, Dr. Zsupan-Jerome is filling a lacuna in the literature regarding Catholic digital communications. Her theological review—written in a style accessible to the average reader—provides a concise analysis of the church's teachings regarding modern social communications, with practical recommendations for digital natives, immigrants, and missionaries. Bishops and academics, pastors and catechists, seminarians and Catholic media professionals, and others will find *Connected toward Communion: The Church and Social Communication in the Digital Age* to be a valuable resource in their ministry."

> —Helen Osman
> Secretary of Communications
> United States Conference of Catholic Bishops

Connected toward Communion

The Church and Social Communication in the Digital Age

Daniella Zsupan-Jerome

A Michael Glazier Book

LITURGICAL PRESS
Collegeville, Minnesota

www.litpress.org

1	2	3	4	5	6	7	8	9

Library of Congress Cataloging-in-Publication Data

Zsupan-Jerome, Daniella.
    Connected toward Communion : the church and social communication in the digital age / Daniella Zsupan-Jerome.
        pages   cm
    "A Michael Glazier book."
    Includes bibliographical references and index.
    ISBN 978-0-8146-8220-3 — ISBN 978-0-8146-8245-6 (ebook)
    1. Communication—Religious aspects—Catholic Church—History.
    2. Church and mass media—History.   I. Title.

    BX1795.C67Z78   2014
    261.5'2—dc23   2014010560

To all communicators of the Word—
may the word of God dwell in us richly in the digital age

CONTENTS

CHURCH AND SOCIAL COMMUNICATION TIMELINE

This timeline, which is not exhaustive, notes some of the key developments in Catholic social communication leading up to the Second Vatican Council and after. It provides a chronological summary of the scope of this study.

1948: Pius XII establishes *ad experimentum* Pontifical Commission for the Study and Ecclesiastical Evaluation of Films on Religious or Moral Subjects.

1948 September 17: *Ad experimentum* commission formalized to become the Pontifical Commission for Educational and Religious Films.

1952: Commission changes to Pontifical Commission for the Cinema.

1954: Commission changes to Pontifical Commission for the Cinema, Radio, and Television.

1957 September: Pius XII issues encyclical *Miranda Prorsus*.

1959 February 22: John XXIII issues motu proprio *Boni Pastoris*, establishes the Pontifical Commission as permanent office.

1960 June 6: John XXIII issues motu proprio *Superno Dei Nutu*, calls for a creation of a preparatory Secretariat for the Press and the Moderation of Shows (SPMS).

1962 August: Secretariat SPMS finalizes and sends out schema "On the Means of Social Communication" to the members of the council. Secretariats reorganized and SPMS subsumed by the Commission for the Lay Apostolate (CLA).

Connected toward CommunionCoCom

1962 November 23–26:The schema on social communication is debated by the Second Vatican Council.

1962 December to **1963** June: Subcommission of CLA works on the revision of the schema.

1963 November 11: Revised document sent to council members.

1963 November 14: Vote on sections of the document. Vote passes.

1963 November 16–17: Two petitions circulate calling for a major revision of document.

1963 November 25: Vote on document as a whole. Vote passes.

1963 December 4: Final and formal vote on the document. Vote passes. Paul VI promulgates the document as conciliar decree *Inter Mirifica*.

1964 April 2: Motu proprio *In Fructibus Multis* renames Pontifical Commission for Film, Radio, and Television to Pontifical Commission for Social Communication. New scope to include the press as well as the whole consideration of social communication for the Church. Commission charged with creating pastoral instruction on social communication.

1964–1971: Pontifical Commission and team of expert consultants work on five revisions of pastoral instruction on social communication.

1967 May 7: Observation of the first World Communication Day.

1971 January 21: Pope Paul VI informally approves pastoral instruction.

1971 May 23–24: Pastoral Instruction *Communio et Progressio* published. President of the Commission, Msgr. Martin O'Connor, disseminates document to bishops worldwide, urges implementation.

1971 June 3: Cardinal Gordon G. Grey of Edinburgh offers public presentation of *Communio et Progessio*.

1977: Congregation for Catholic Education commissions study on seminary formation in social communication.

1986 March 19: Congregation for Catholic Education publishes *Guide to the Training of Future Priests Concerning the Instruments of Social Communication*.

1987: Plenary Assembly of Pontifical Commission for Social Communication explores the question of adding a commemorative supplement to *Communio et Progressio*.

1988 –1992: Commission and expert consultants work on *Aetatis Novae*.

1989 March 1: Pontifical Commission for Social Communication becomes Pontifical Council.

1990 January 24: World Communications Day Message addresses "The Christian Message in a Computer Culture," first among the messages with this specific focus.

1992 February 22: *Aetatis Novae*, Pastoral Instruction commemorating twentieth anniversary of *Communio et Progressio* published.

1995 December 25: The website www.vatican.va becomes active.

2001 January 24: World Communications Day Message addresses digital media in "Preach from the Housetops: The Gospel in the Age of Global Communication."

2002 February 22: Pontifical Council for Social Communication publishes *Ethics in Internet* and *Church and Internet*.

2002 January 24: World Communications Day Message focuses on "The Internet: A New Forum for Proclaiming the Gospel."

2005 January 24: John Paul II offers Apostolic Letter *The Rapid Development*, his last document.

2009: World Communications Day Messages begin to consistently address digital media and digital culture.

2012 December: Papal Twitter account @Pontifex launched.

2013 January: The Pope App is released.

PREFACE

In the spirit of evangelization, this study aims to bring good news to all pastoral ministers about the gift and challenge of digital communication. No longer just tools and instruments, the digital media have created a cultural milieu in which how we communicate, gain understanding, and relate to one another is changing. In the midst of these cultural changes, the Church's fundamental evangelizing mission remains the same: the great commission to proclaim the Gospel of Jesus Christ to all the world. As communication is essential to the Church's identity, the present cultural shift marked by the digital media is of utmost importance as it touches all of the Church's ministerial activity, on a global and local level. From the curial offices of the Vatican to the parish youth minister, we are all thinking about how to help make present the Gospel message in this emerging culture.

To experience a cultural shift is overwhelming, exciting, and challenging. In light of this, the good news this study bears is that of tradition. The Church has thought consistently about the gift and challenge of social communication for decades, beginning a systematic development of a social communication tradition with the Second Vatican Council's document *Inter Mirifica* (the Decree on the Mass Media). In the decades since Vatican II, the Church's reflection continued with the pastoral instructions *Communio et Progressio* and *Aetatis Novae*; shorter documents on Church, internet, and ethics; apostolic letters such as *The Rapid Development*; practical guides on formation; and a long line of World Communications Day messages. In addition to documents, the Church also teaches through practice, especially as digital media have become part and parcel of the practical activity of the Church today. This study surveys this social communication tradition with an eye toward the formation of the pastoral minister for serving in our digital culture.

True to the ethos of digital culture, this study needs conversation partners to continue the reflection and keep facilitating the dialogue between tradition, culture, and the Church's evangelizing task. One salient area for further exploration is the thematic thrust of the World Communication Day Messages, which have since 1967 sustained the social communications conversation and have more recently assumed the reality of digital culture as a consistent context for reflection; this study offers a summary but sees an opportunity for elaboration.

This study stands on the shoulders of the documents and practices of the Church's social communication tradition, and I am grateful for the invaluable heritage they present for our digital culture. I am also grateful to a network of generous mentors, companions, and colleagues who have encouraged and supported this study: Dr. Tom Ryan, director of the Loyola Institute for Ministry and all of my colleagues there who have helped me balance teaching and work while writing this book; my generous, deep, and passionate students at Loyola who have thought with me; Loyola University New Orleans for supporting my travel to Rome; Helen and John Osman, Fr. Paul Soukup, SJ, and Fr. Antonio Spadaro, SJ, for your mentorship, wisdom, and example; colleagues who have gathered at TheoCom in Santa Clara for your inspiration; and the United States Conference of Catholic Bishops Communications Committee for inviting me into the conversation.

The final chapter of this book owes its research to my travel to Rome during the spring of 2014, and I am much indebted to the Pontifical Council for Social Communications for their hospitality and generosity in sharing their insights and experiences with digital media: Archbishop Claudio Maria Celli, Monsignor Paul Tighe, T. J. Jones, Fr. Ariel Beramendi, Fr. Janvier Yameogo, and all the staff I had the pleasure of meeting there. Thank you also to Greg Burke of the Secretariat of State, Frank Rocca of Catholic News Service, and Fr. Joseph Fowler of the North American College for the opportunity for a conversation while there.

Hálás köszönet for the love and support of my family, who were companions, conversation partners, and fellow travelers along the way. For Randy and Fitz, my domestic Church—*deo gratias*.

Finally, I prayerfully express my gratitude to God for bringing this work to completion. I hope for the word of God to dwell in us richly in the digital age.

Daniella Zsupan-Jerome

INTRODUCTION

Culture is in a state of constant flux. And if you don't know what is happening today, you are outside of it.[1] This pithy statement on *Wired* magazine's website sums up the dynamism, excitement, and pressure of our digital culture, a combination that leaves many lay and ordained ministers unsettled or even overwhelmed. How the digital media have saturated our culture is increasingly relevant for all contexts of communication today, including the Church in all of its local and universal manifestations. The gadgets that we and those we serve carry around have connected us in new ways, while distancing us in some others. Ministry professionals may wonder (or stress about) what is the best way to reach congregations, groups, and the people they serve, including those mysterious "digital natives" who are young enough that their world has always included internet-mediated communication. Beyond these, we wonder about how the Church can reach beyond her walls with the help of digital communication to be present to those who have left, who have lost interest, who are perhaps angry, or who have never been interested in the first place. The potential for being present through the digital media to those in and outside of the Church is exciting territory, inviting more and more exploration from those in ministry.

At the same time, exploring the digital media for ministry requires the time, skill set, and resources to do it well. Investing in digital

---

1. See wired.com, http://www.wired.com/underwire/2013/08/101signals -culture/, accessed April 7, 2014.

media ministry is a real commitment. As *Wired* reminds us, these media are part of a culture that is in a constant state of flux. Technologies change, hardware and gadgets need updating and replacement, and establishing a vibrant online presence demands time, regular attention, and flexibility to move on to the next platform, if that is where people are. Sensing this commitment, many ministry professionals get overwhelmed or back away from exploring the digital possibilities of their ministry. As a result, many in ministry are caught in the uneasy place of sensing that we are in the throes of an immense cultural change, but unsure of how to participate in it manageably and effectively toward serving the reign of God.

Wired magazine's pithy statement above perpetuates a myth in hinting that what is culturally relevant is also what is most up-to-date. While the digital culture does indeed uphold "the latest" as one of its values, communication overall is a cultural reality that is as old as human relationality itself. It is a concept that involves the bodily, the symbolic, and the artistic, as well as the textual. From a theological point of view, it is a concept that invites us into the very mystery of God who is Father, Son, and Spirit in mutual and self-giving communication, and who communicates with humankind through the movement of revelation throughout history. This revelation culminates in the incarnation of *the Word*, who communicates salvation through his life, death, and resurrection. After him, communication of his good news becomes the Spirit-led task of the Church. This age-old mission to communicate is at the heart of the Church. From this perspective, the digital media are but the latest chapter in the long story of how the Church has gone about expressing this identity and mission to communicate.

This is a steady foundation for those in ministry, one that can alleviate the pressure that comes from being otherwise rooted in the dynamic reality of digital culture itself. As ministers of the Church, the task of communication is integral to the mission at hand. The Church has collective wisdom in this task for exploring the way forward in the digital age. This study invites readers into this reservoir of ecclesial teachings and practices, as it especially pertains to engaging in ministry in the digital age in and through internet-mediated communication. In special focus of this study are the social communication teachings and practices of the Church since the Second Vatican Council.

Making a Case for Social Communication

On November 24, 1962, during the first session of the Second Vatican Council, Archbishop Rene Louis Marie Stroum of Sens, France, addressed the council members gathered in the nave of St. Peter's Basilica to begin their discussion of the topic of social communication. To make his case about the importance of this topic, Archbishop Stroum offered some numbers: around the world in 1962, there were 8,000 daily newspapers with a circulation of 300 million, 22,000 periodicals with a circulation of 200 million, 2,500 films produced annually seen 17 billion times, 600 broadcasting stations with an audience of 400 million, and 1,000 television stations reaching an audience of 120 million.[2] Tallying this up yields that the print and broadcast media were accessed 18 billion times. In exploring the topic of social communication, the council fathers recognized an increasingly powerful cultural phenomenon whereby the sharing of information was taking place at a massive scale. Being aware that information and ideas shared with a massive audience had the power to shape the mind, and indeed, culture itself, the council elevated in importance this topic, eventually producing and promulgating the decree *Inter Mirifica* as one of the sixteen documents of Vatican II.

Fifty plus years after the promulgation of this conciliar decree, the question of social communication has grown to define the culture of our digital age. As compared to the reach of the mass media in 1962, 2.8 billion people (39 percent of today's global population) access the internet, a social communications medium that was not available to the public at the time of the council.[3] Considering those numbers, along with the continuing reach of print and broadcast media (media one does not access through the internet), social communication is now a cultural force that shapes our day-to-day lives in new and constantly changing ways. Recognizing social communication and all of its innovative technologies as a cultural force does not mean that it is a distinct entity apart from the Church. In fact, since the promulgation

2. Norman Tanner, *The Church and the World: Gaudium et Spes, Inter Mirifica* (Mahwah, NJ: Paulist Press, 2005), 97.

3. Statistic provided for 2013 by the International Telecommunications Union; see http://www.itu.int, accessed April 7, 2014.

of *Inter Mirifica*, the past five decades have seen regular attention to the topic of social communication in the forms of ecclesial documents and, more recently, digital communication practices. Papal presence on social media and communication of Church news through mobile media applications are the most recent chapters in the story of how the Church has approached the task and mission of communicating faith in the digital age.

Communicating Church

As noted above, the task of communication is integral to the Church. To claim then that the Church's thought on social communication stems from *Inter Mirifica* would be viewing the topic through too narrow a lens, both from the theological approach to communication and from the Church's self-understanding of her mission and her task. The Church communicates, both in her identity as the Body of Christ the Word incarnate, and in her task of proclaiming the Good News to all the earth (Mark 16:15). For theologians such as Avery Dulles and Franz-Josef Eilers, this communication comes from the movement at the very heart of the Trinity; it is the dynamic of revelation, it is expressed in fullness in the incarnation of the Word, and it becomes the task of the Church.[4] Since the Spirit empowered those gathered on Pentecost Day in the Upper Room to go and speak of the Gospel to the pilgrims in Jerusalem, the Church has been fundamentally concerned with the communication of the Good News of Jesus Christ. Media for communicating the Good News have also been integral to this evangelizing task: preaching and letter writing brought the message of the Gospel to the early Church, handwritten codices presented and preserved the Word in later centuries, slowly giving way to the printed word. From the perspective of communication, it is a powerful anecdote of history that the first printed volume on Gutenberg's press was a Bible. The twentieth century saw the broad-

---

4. See Franz-Josef Eilers, *Communicating in Ministry and Mission*, 3rd ed. (Manila, Philippines: Logos, 2009); Avery Robert Dulles, "Vatican II and Communications," in *Vatican II Assessment and Perspectives Twenty-Five Years After (1962–1987)*, ed. Rene Latourelle, vol. 3 (Mahwah, NJ: Paulist Press, 1989), 528–47.

ening of communications media from print to the electronic—radio, television, film—and the Gospel found its unique expression through each of these. From the end of the twentieth century to the beginning of the twenty-first, we have experienced the rise of the digital media. Fruitful engagement with this media will be the next chapter in the Church's long history of social communication.[5]

When *Inter Mirifica* and the subsequent pastoral instruction *Communio et Progressio* (1971) were crafted, the term "social communication" brought to mind broadcast media such as print journalism, television and radio, film, and even theater to some extent. On the twentieth anniversary of *Communio et Progressio*, the pastoral instruction *Aetatis Novae* (1992) is first among these documents to mention computer networks, a medium that will merit its own documents a decade later (*Church and Internet* and *Ethics in Internet*, both published in 2002). In our present day, social communication is a term that continues to imply the traditional broadcast media, but it increasingly bears a closer association with the digital media and internet-mediated communication.[6] For social communication, the significance of the internet also ushers in new assumptions about communication on this massive scale. Social communication through the traditional broadcast media implies a one-to-many model of sharing information: there is a clear source of information and a clear audience who receives it. Social communication through the internet, especially since the advent of Web 2.0 technologies, reshapes this one-to-many

5. The brief overview of various media presented here is incomplete. In addition to media that focus on the verbal, considering the nonverbal, visual, embodied, performative, and ritual expressions of communication rounds out this picture. The history of Christian art presents a variety of other media that communicate the Good News in a spectrum of ways. Theater and performance are also media with a long history in Christian tradition. The liturgy itself has a ritual and symbolic language that communicates the Good News in a particular way. A full treatment of Christian media will thus consider the verbal, visual, embodied, performative, ritual, and sacramental languages of the tradition.

6. Media commentators have noted the gradual decline of print and other broadcast media, measured in advertising revenue, circulation, cumulative audience, and similar standards. Online media, on the other hand, are on a slight and steady rise, especially as many broadcasting outlets are broadening their reach to the digital audiences. See http://stateofthemedia.org/, accessed April 7, 2014.

model into an interactive web. Internet-mediated communication since the rise of social media and mobile media applications has become a chorus of many voices who coparticipate in the creation, sharing, and dissemination of information. In addition to the grand-scale participation of the author-audience, the internet also grants freedom and flexibility for people to piece the information they gather together according to their own interests and preferences. Mobile media applications (apps) are especially effective in enabling people to glean from the flow of information only what is relevant and interesting to them. In the digital age, the audience has also become author and publisher, as well as agent of what information reaches them.[7]

The full implications of this shift are far from being determined; at best, we can enter into an ongoing dialogue with these cultural developments as they continue to unfold. This study intends to contribute to this ongoing dialogue, especially focusing on the internet as the dominant social communication medium of our digital age. Exploring what is new is at once daunting and exhilarating. From the perspective of theological scholarship, the digital media continue to raise pertinent questions about ontology, epistemology, morality, and ethics: being, knowing, and being together in this digital age. From a pastoral perspective, figuring out how to incorporate social and other digital media into ministerial practice is the lingering question of the day, especially as digital technologies continue to shape the way we communicate into something new. Yet the question is broader: rather than incorporating digital technologies into ministry, the greater challenge is to perceive and understand ministry as embedded in a new culture shaped profoundly by digital communication. For those forging ahead on this ministerial path, this study offers a systematic overview of the Church's approach to the question of social communication. Focusing on the Second Vatican Council and thereafter, this book pauses with each of the key social communication docu-

7. This rhetorical statement intends to illustrate the nature of the social web. Internet data-mining, online advertising methods, and efforts by companies to profile their digital consumer are significant factors that also shape the information we encounter online. For media commentators who warn against these, see, for example, Nicholas Carr, *The Shallows* (New York: W. W. Norton, 2011) and Jaron Lanier, *You Are Not a Gadget* (New York: Alfred Knopf, 2010).

ments since the council, and then considers some of the more recent communications practices of the Church. The result is a study that distills some of the key points and positions on the questions of social communication, offering familiar markers for charting the unfamiliar road that lies ahead in the realm of the digital media.

One challenge to approaching digital media studies in a systematic way is that these media are indeed fluid and quickly changing with the advancement of communication technologies. The digital media tell an unfinished story, the narrative of which is at the same time powerfully reshaping how we communicate, including how we approach the finding, evaluating, understanding, and sharing of information. Gaining knowledge and accepting information as authentic, trustworthy, and true is a process that the digital media have radically augmented: knowledge and all of these aspects of it are increasingly participatory, user generated, collaborative, and rooted in the social network.[8] Top-down, single source information now finds (or loses) itself in a cacophony of comments, opinions, perspectives. In the social network, who said it and what they said seems to matter less than how many people converged around the information at hand or participated in the process of sharing that information. Going "viral" is the authentication of a new form of authority, albeit a fleeting one, quickly replaced by the next digital trend.

At the same time, authoritative voices of the traditional kind do remain. As of early 2014, 13 million people follow @Pontifex, the papal Twitter account, clear evidence that who Pope Francis is and what he says still matters. What has changed with the advent of the digital media is how people are able to interact with the information that arrives from traditional sources of authority. Following @Pontifex, one has the choice to appreciate, respect, disagree with, or even debase the papal messages, and to publicly manifest this choice through the sharing of one's comments connected to each papal tweet. A papal tweet and messages ranging from affirmation to profanity share the same visual space, all making up the overall message on the screen. In the digital culture, our experience and

---

8. For an overview of participatory culture and the digital media, see Henry Jenkins, et al., *Confronting the Challenges of Participatory Culture: Media Education for the 21st Century* (Cambridge, MA: MIT Press, 2009).

understanding of authority is shifting. This shift, as is the case for so much of digital media, is difficult to pin down and to fully define. As the digital communication continues to evolve, perhaps a more useful image for the moment is that of the pendulum, swinging from two opposite ends but remaining in touch with both.

Both remaining in touch with the traditional and welcoming what is new is the blessed challenge of pastoral theology and ministry, especially when it comes to digital culture. Both/ands are often co-nundrums that force the exploration of how two realties that are seemingly opposite in fact fit together, and for ministry, they are blessed challenges often out of which something truly creative can emerge. Both/ands are also familiar and integral to many of the beliefs and concepts at the heart of Catholic theology: Christ human and divine, the paschal mystery as death and resurrection, the risen Lord as present and absent, sacrament as tangible and transcen-dent, the Church as local and universal, the people of God as saints and sinners, the Body of Christ as one and many. The Catholic and Christian tradition overall invites a liminal existence, in the tension of the both/and, the already and the not yet. Theologically at least, we know the both/and, and pastorally, the transitional time we are living in our digital culture is a new opportunity for living this the-ology. The challenge is figuring out how to navigate this particular transition in this particular cultural context, holding both tradition and innovation in hand.

The topic of social communication can be a daunting one for pas-toral workers and theological thinkers. By nature difficult to conclu-sively define but at the same time increasingly pervasive and relevant for our culture, social communication compels many of us to scramble to incorporate digital media practices into our ministries, while not fully exploring why or how to do so faithfully. This tendency is not new: accounts of the discussion of the council fathers in 1962, as they spent two and a half days on the subject, reveal the same tension. Their comments on the subject consistently revealed a sense of the subject's relevance, but they also lacked a systematic approach or a way to synthesize the question. The result of their work, *Inter Mirifica*, was an invitation to think more on the subject. This continued thought and practice is evidenced in the work of the Pontifical Council for Social Communication in documents such as *Communio et Progressio*

(1971), *Aetatis Novae* (1992), *The Church and Internet* (2002), and *Ethics in Internet* (2002).[9] Parallel to these are documents such as the Congregation for Catholic Education's *Guide to the Instruction of Future Priests Concerning the Instruments of Social Communication* (1986), and John Paul II's *The Rapid Development* (2005), just two examples of the Church's broadening awareness and concern about media and faith. Alongside this whole trajectory is the establishment of World Communication Day and the series of papal messages published for each since 1967 as an ongoing exploration of the question of social communication. Finally, the witness of the Church in digital communication, such as its presence online, in social networking, and through mobile media applications also manifests the Church's ongoing engagement with the question of social communication and reveals the Church's implicit understanding on the topic. The explicit and implicit teaching present in these works and examples offers guidance to the greater Church as well as a foundation out of which to think, explore, and minister as the media of our time continue to evolve.

Formation for Ministry in the Digital Age

This foundation is, however, neither a synthesis nor a once-and-for-all assessment of digital media from the perspective of faith. What the Church's explicit and implicit teaching on this topic offers instead is a basis for ongoing dialogue and exploration of how the means of social communication continue to shape culture, and how the Church can continue effectively to exercise her fundamental task of evangelization in this changing context. This basis is one of ongoing ambiguity and opportunity, challenge and frustration, marvel and excitement. In addition to existing in this ongoing state of exploration, there are other real and practical challenges to effective social communication for faith: resources, materials, personnel, and technical

---

9. Between 1992 and 2002, the Pontifical Council for Social Communication worked specifically on the question of ethics: *Ethics in Advertising* (1997), *Ethics in Communication* (2000), and finally, *Ethics in Internet* (2002), a companion to *Church and Internet*. These documents are important but beyond the scope of this present work.

know-how. Given all of these, *Inter Mirifica* called for formation of all lay and ordained ministers "to acquire the competence needed to use the media for the apostolate."[10] Formation is also the term echoed by the Pontifical Council for Social Communication (PCCS) today as it continues to explore this topic from a practical perspective for the good of the Church. According to Archbishop Claudio Celli, president of the PCCS:

> Formation is essential for developing and laying a solid foundation for the Church's communications ministry. If we are to proclaim the Good News of Jesus Christ through our personal witness and our professional work in the media, if we want to promote true reconciliation, justice and peace, we must have communicators who are properly formed in Christian values and morals, and not only professionally trained in communication techniques and technology.[11]

Along these lines, this study will use the concept of formation as a specific lens for examining the Church's teaching about social communication since the Second Vatican Council. In examining key documents and practices since Vatican II, we will especially consider how the explicit and implicit teachings of the Church aim to be formative for personal witness and professional work in the Church. By using this lens, this study will help readers gather what the Church teaches about social communication, as well as offer them practical steps for engaging with the digital media. Such engagement is necessary not only out of practical necessity but also out of the shared mission of the Church to communicate the Good News in word, deed, and witness of life.

What is meant by formation?[12] In a sense, this term is broadly applicable to the nurturing of Christian identity. Formation is part of the language of articulating the task of catechesis, the process by

10. IM 15.

11. Claudio Maria Celli, "Social Communication," *AFER* 51, no. 3 (September 1, 2009): 188.

12. The concept of formation is broadly applicable for multiple forms and contexts of religious education. For this present study, the focus remains on the nurturing of ministers for service of the Church. For an overview of different approaches to and understanding of formation, see Paul Overend, "Education or

which believers are nurtured toward conversion of mind and heart to Jesus Christ.[13] Likewise, formation also describes the nurturing of those called to the religious or consecrated life, as well as professional ministerial identity, such as toward priesthood and lay ecclesial ministry. For the purpose if this study, formation will imply this latter category, focusing especially on those in professional ministry who seek to integrate effective social communication practices into their work.

The Second Vatican Council treated the question of professional ministerial formation most specifically in *Optatam Totius*, the 1965 decree on the training of priests, and to a lesser extent in *Apostolicam Actuositatem*, the 1965 decree on the apostolate of the laity.[14] In the decades since the council, the Church has reflected on such professional formation from a broader ministerial perspective, including priestly formation and the formation of those called to lay ecclesial ministry.[15] The goals and guidance set for both priestly and lay ecclesial ministry formation envision a fourfold approach of edifying the human, spiritual, intellectual, and pastoral capacities of persons called to ministry.[16] These four categories of formation will also help to frame the lens by which this study will examine the formative aspects of the Church's teaching on social communication. In studying the Church's social communications documents and practices, elements that seek to edify the human, spiritual, intellectual, and pastoral capacities

---

Formation? The Issue of Personhood in Learning for Ministry," *Journal of Adult Theological Education* 4, no. 2 (2007): 133–48.

13. See, for instance, *General Directory for Catechesis* (Washington, DC: USCCB Publishing, 1998), 25.

14. In terms of a treatment of formation, *Optatam Totius* provides a more systematic approach, already naming the four elements that John Paul II will later flesh out in *Pastores Dabo Vobis*. *Apostolicam Actuositatem* acknowledges the need for the training toward the apostolate in more general terms. See AA 28–33.

15. In the United States, two key documents to illustrate this are *The Program of Priestly Formation* (2006) and *Co-Workers in the Vineyard of the Lord* (2005).

16. See John Paul II's 1992 Apostolic Exhortation *Pastores Dabo Vobis*, paragraphs 43–59; *Program of Priestly Formation*, 28–84; *Co-Workers*, 33–49. *Optatam Totius* already names the need for spiritual (8–12), intellectual (13–18), and pastoral training (19–20), along with formation toward human maturity (11). *Pastores Dabo Vobis* distills these four toward a systematic plan.

will receive special note. With an eye toward our digital context, the reality of a changing culture of communication shaping all four of these pillars in new ways presents new questions, opportunities, and challenges for ministerial formation today.

A full treatment of each of these four elements is beyond the scope of this work, but they are fleshed out in John Paul II's *Pastores Dabo Vobis* (1992), the post-synodal apostolic exhortation on priestly formation, as well as subsequent priestly and lay ecclesial formation plans, *Program of Priestly Formation* (2006) and *Co-Workers in the Vineyard of the Lord* (2005), both created to guide ministerial formation in the United States. In order to better understand the formative potential of the Church's teaching on social communication, each of the four main pillars of ministerial formation contain key aspects relevant for social communication and for approaching ministry in the digital age. Along these lines, this study proposes a departure from an overly practical understanding of communication perceived solely as a pastoral skill, such as training for how to handle an interview or preside at a televised liturgy. In the cultural shift wrought by digital communication, social communication raises broader questions under all four pillars.

Human Formation

Human formation aims to develop the minister's capacity to relate to those around them, especially those they serve in their professional context. According to *Pastores Dabo Vobis*, the goal of effective human formation for ministry is for the minister's personality to serve as a bridge for others in their meeting with Jesus Christ, the Redeemer of humanity.[17] Along these lines, *Co-Workers in the Vineyard* similarly emphasizes human qualities such as character and a healthy and well-balanced personality for the sake of personal growth and ministerial service.[18] Relevant for this study of social communication is the emphasis that Church teaching on human formation places on the minister's capacity to relate to others in terms of community and communion. According to *Pastores Dabo Vobis*:

17. John Paul II, *Pastores Dabo Vobis*, 43.
18. *Co-Workers*, 36.

This is truly fundamental for a person who is called to be responsible for a community and to be a "man of communion." This demands that the priest not be arrogant, or quarrelsome, but affable, hospitable, sincere in his words and heart, prudent and discreet, generous and ready to serve, capable of opening himself to clear and brotherly relationships and of encouraging the same in others, and quick to understand, forgive and console (125) (cf. 1 Tim 3:1-5; Titus 1:7-9). People today are often trapped in situations of standardization and loneliness, especially in large urban centers, and they become ever more appreciative of the value of communion. Today this is one of the most eloquent signs and one of the most effective ways of transmitting the Gospel message.[19]

Communicating to relate with others and bring them toward community and communion is a quality that is highlighted anew by the digital context; according to Msgr. Paul Tighe, the question of formation for communication needs to begin here.[20] Internet-mediated communication paradoxically connects and isolates: we can connect with anyone on the World Wide Web, but our mutual presence is mediated by the tools available to us. Conveying presence online entails a range of options, from textual and asynchronous communication such as e-mail, to audiovisual and synchronous communication, such as live web conferencing. Where our communication falls within this range shapes the presence we convey. As the technologies evolve, our presence can become increasingly media rich yet remain qualitatively different than what we experience with one another face-to-face. Mediated presence poses a key question for formation in the digital age, challenging us to think about how we can maintain relationships, develop new ones, and ensure that we can continue to be available to the people to whom we should be present.[21] Human formation in the digital age thus involves the minister's capacity to be present to the people he or she serves, with an ecology of options to convey presence. These dynamics of human relationality in the digital context raise new questions for what it means to communicate toward

19. John Paul II, *Pastores Dabo Vobis*, 43.
20. Paul Tighe, secretary of the Pontifical Council for Social Communications, personal interview, February 18, 2014.
21. Ibid.

community and communion. As this study explores the Church's teachings on social communications, the question of human formation for relating authentically in the digital age will prove critical.

Spiritual Formation

Spiritual formation is essential to the overall formation of the professional minister; in fact *Pastores Dabo Vobis* considers spiritual formation as the completion of human formation.[22] Along these lines, spiritual formation elevates human relationality to human-divine relationality. It invites the professional minister into its very source: the mystery of the Trinity.[23] While much focus is placed on developing an interiority for ministry, spiritual formation in fact entails community: it assumes that the human person's innate search for God is a search for Christ that is inherited from and nurtured by the Church community. Praying with the word, participating in the liturgy, and engaging in service are essential to this process.[24]

From the perspective of social communication, commitment to spiritual formation calls us to assess the potential of the digital media for facilitating the interior search for God toward the encounter with Christ, ultimately expressed in the context of the worshiping community.[25] Spiritual formation in the digital age challenges us to discern and seek spaces for solitude and silence as part and parcel of our digital culture rather than apart from it, so that our presence to one another can be authentic and manifest God's presence through real relationships.[26] More specifically, it asks whether digital communication practices can image the pattern of human-divine communication that is rooted in the

22. John Paul II, *Pastores Dabo Vobis*, 45.
23. See *Optatam Totius* 8, *Pastores Dabo Vobis*, 45.
24. John Paul II, *Pastores Dabo Vobis*, 46.
25. This approach here aims to be consistent with the articulation of and vision for professional ministry in the Roman Catholic context. The topic of online religion and spirituality as a whole also includes a variety of other assumptions and understandings of how spirituality and Internet-mediated communication intersect, challenge, and/or enhance one another. See Heidi Campbell, *Exploring Religious Community Online* (New York: Peter Lang, 2005).
26. Paul Tighe, secretary of the Pontifical Council for Social Communications, personal interview, February 18, 2014.

life of the Trinity. Franz-Josef Eilers notes regarding ministerial formation overall that it necessarily implies a process that "affects the whole person and his/her basic inner disposition."[27] For social communication toward ministry, according to Eilers, this inner disposition must be capable of the "giving of self in love" in image of the very dynamic of the Trinity that generates the Christian concept of communication.[28] The nurturing of an inner disposition from which the minister authentically gives oneself in love speaks to the spiritual formation pillar most directly. Forming and living out this disposition can be challenging in the digital context, especially in terms of maintaining good ministerial boundaries. In the digital context, the skill of presenting oneself authentically while at the same time maintaining appropriate boundaries is a standard that finds itself in the midst of a whole range of experimentation with self-presentation. From the intentional creation of a profile page to representing oneself through an avatar, the giving of oneself online happens in a host of ways. Similarly, boundaries are tested as personal information becomes simultaneously public when shared online. With this in mind, this study will highlight what the Church's teaching and practices offer toward the spiritual formation of those engaging in ministry in and through the digital media.

Intellectual Formation

Intellectual formation toward professional ministry aims to enable a greater understanding of the content of faith and the capacity to articulate it truthfully so that others may also grow in understanding as well. Its ultimate hope is "to participate in the light of God's mind" as it "seeks to acquire wisdom which in turn opens to and is directed toward knowing and adhering to God."[29] From the perspective of the ecclesial task of communicating faith, intellectual formation is important for the process of revelation, and for the human person's effective participation in the transmission of the content of faith.

The digital media of social communication offer significant opportunities and challenges for the task of intellectual formation toward

---

27. Eilers, *Communicating in Ministry and Mission*, 157.
28. Ibid.
29. John Paul II, *Pastores Dabo Vobis*, 51.

ministry. In digital culture, education and the role of the teacher shifts as a whole, from a gatekeeper or dispenser of knowledge to a guide who accompanies the learner and offers a frame of reference or criteria for judging and interpreting content.[30] Teaching as dispensing content no longer dominates; the digital media offer access to information at an unprecedented scale. The sheer quantity of information available is an undeniable gift for learning, research, and other intellectual pursuits, and it broadens the possibility for access beyond the classroom. On the other hand, not all information is the same. It can be challenging to evaluate information online (or its source) as authentic, trustworthy, and true. Teaching as guiding becomes relevant here, as learning to evaluate information online is part of an overall digital media literacy that is necessary for effective social communication. This study will examine the Church's teachings on social communication with an eye toward what these teachings might offer toward greater digital media literacy for ministry.

Pastoral Formation

Pastoral formation for lay and ordained ministers emerges from practical theology and implies action that is rooted in, grows from, and returns to theological reflection. Pastoral formation envisions the minister in his or her professional role, and thus seeks to enhance the knowledge, skills, and attitudes necessary for this.[31] This professional role is often, in some sense, a role of leadership or a role or collaboration with other professionals toward a common effort in ministry, and above all seeks the building of community. For the priestly ministry, *Pastores Dabo Vobis* offers the biblical image of the good shepherd as the metaphor for the priest's pastoral role.[32] For lay and ordained professional ministers, pastoral formation entails and incorporates more than good leadership and administrative skills. Exercising one's pastoral role is always a public, ecclesial task that represents Christ's own servant leadership in and for the community.

30. Paul Tighe, secretary of the Pontifical Council for Social Communications, personal interview, February 18, 2014.

31. *Co-Workers*, 49.

32. John Paul II, *Pastores Dabo Vobis*, 57.

In terms of social communication, the pastoral aspect of formation offers the opportunity and challenge for ministerial professionals to guide and serve people online. This poses the question of not just whether to be present online, but how to be present in a way that will lead people to encounter Jesus Christ, here represented through how the minister exercises the public and ecclesial role of servant leadership, especially in communication. Integral to this is building community: not only to offer presence to individuals but also to foster relationships in the community by getting others to communicate as well.[33] In addition to relationality on a communal level, exercising the public voice, serving as thought-leader, and exemplifying good digital citizenship practices are some of the practical skills and tasks that fall under this aspect of formation.[34] As practical theology also invites ministers to be reflectively rooted in the revealed Word of God, a challenge for pastoral formation toward an online ministerial presence is how to incorporate a consistent method of critical reflection into their pastoral work online. As Nicholas Carr warns in *The Shallows* (2011), the internet is a medium that scatters the attention, and could in fact hinder deep, sustained, reflective, and creative thought. While Carr's warnings are contested, his observation about the pace and focus (or lack of focus) of our online activities is worth considering.[35] This study proceeds with an eye toward what the Church's teachings on social communication offer for pastoral formation along these lines in the digital context.

Do Not Be Afraid

Each time I begin a new semester of online or hybrid teaching, I encourage students with these scriptural words. Most of my students at the Loyola Institute for Ministry are already either professional

33. Paul Tighe, secretary of the Pontifical Council for Social Communications, personal interview, February 18, 2014.

34. Elizabeth Drescher describes online ministerial presence through social media such as blogging as "thought-leadership." See Drescher and Anderson. *Click 2 Save: The Digital Ministry Bible* (New York: Morehouse, 2012), 94–95.

35. For a different and more optimistic interpretation of the cognitive effects of internet-mediated communication, see, for instance, Cathy Davidson, *Now You See It* (New York: Penguin, 2012).

ministers or hoping to pursue this path, and many of my assign-
ments require the students to explore the digital media for ministry.
Oftentimes, even the students thoroughly versed in the internet and
digital media in general are new to both online learning and the exploration of digital media ministry resources. *Do not be afraid* is more
than just a generally applicable truth from the wisdom of Scripture.
It is a phrase that roots Christian ministers today in the tradition
that has preceded them for millennia. It is a phrase that resounds in
Scripture dozens of times, from Genesis to Revelation. In the Gospel
of John, it is among the risen Lord's parting words as he entrusts his
ministry to his followers. And in the popular Catholic theology of
the late twentieth and early twenty-first centuries, it is a phrase that
Pope John Paul II used over and over again in his messages to the
Church and the world. *The Rapid Development*, his last apostolic letter
and one that addresses social communication in the digital age, ends
by vehemently echoing this phrase. It is tradition, past and present.

Evoking this sense of tradition is intentional. Overwhelmed,
daunted, challenged, intrigued, and enthusiastic are just a few ways
to describe the complex mind-set of those facing the digital media
with a professional ministerial aim for the first time. Reminding these
learners of the tradition as a long-standing and sure foundation for
what they set out to do is the symbol of my encouragement for them
in the beginning of a course. I offer this study to readers in the same
spirit. Do not be afraid of this unknown, overwhelming, evolving,
dangerous, marvelous, and awesome medium, a medium that, in the
words of Paul VI, "human skill is daily rendering more perfect."[36] The
wisdom of the tradition, the guidance of the Spirit, and fruitful dialogue between faith and culture will pave the way on this new path.

---

36. Paul VI, *Evangelii Nuntiandi*, 45.

1 BEGINNING THE CONVERSATION

Inter Mirifica: The Decree on the Mass Media (1963)

As the introduction points out, the story of the Church's teaching on communications did not begin with the conciliar decree *Inter Mirifica*. In fact, the conciliar decree did not even mark the first time the Church offered teaching on the means of social communication in a modern sense; Pope Pius XII's *Miranda Prorsus*, predating the council by six years, is an encyclical similar in focus to *Inter Mirifica*.[1] Yet the consideration of social communication at a conciliar level elevates this topic in importance in such a way that *Inter Mirifica* became a benchmark document for contemporary discussions of Church teaching on social communication. In addition to *Inter Mirifica*'s status as

---

1. For an overview of the history of the Church' teaching on social communication, see Franz-Josef Eilers, *Communicating Church: Social Communication Documents* (Manila, Philippines: Logos, 2011). For a summary of the Church teaching on the media in the decades leading up to Vatican II, see Matthew E. Bunson, "The History and Development of Post-Conciliar Catholic Social Communications," in *Foundation Theology 2007: Student Essays for Ministry Professionals* (South Bend, IN: Cloverdale, 2007), 206–7. For a bibliographic overview of ecclesial documents and commentaries that touch on the topic of communication, see Paul A. Soukup, *Christian Communication: A Bibliographical Survey*, ed. G. E. Gorman, vol. 14 (New York: Greenwood Press, 1989), 79–91.

a conciliar decree, the council itself that generated it added to the overall relevance of this document for social communication, and what we may learn from it for our digital culture. Although *Inter Mirifica* predates the clarity the council came to in its later discussion of the Church and the modern world communicated in the pastoral constitution *Gaudium et Spes*, Bishop Walther Kampe asserts that the decree should still be read in the spirit of *Gaudium et Spes*, a spirit that "entails a positive attitude on the part of the Church towards human activity and achievement," and a spirit that came eventually to define Vatican II.[2]

The Second Vatican Council's status as a watershed moment for the Church in the twentieth century has been treated extensively in scholarly literature.[3] Key words to describe the spirit of the council include renewal, reform, aggiornamento (updating), openness, dialogue, and reading the signs of the times. It is significant that the Church entered into conversation regarding the topic of social communication in this spirit. Wisely recognizing the cultural shifts occurring around this topic, the Church began a conversation, seeking to find wisdom moving forward as these new media continued to shape the world.

Along these lines, *Inter Mirifica* is less systematic and instead more engaged in the ongoing observation of the means of social communication, offering moral and pastoral entry points for the voice of faith and beginning a dialogue with this aspect of culture so that humankind may ultimately flourish through its use. This stance, which was much critiqued at the time of the decree's promulgation for not offering more definitive teaching on communication can be viewed as providential for today's ecclesial approach toward social communication as it leaves the conversation open to the evolution of the media and the digital culture of communication generated by it.

Andre Ruszkowski, SJ, names *Inter Mirifica* the most criticized yet least known and understood document of the Second Vatican

---

2. Walther Kampe, "Communicating with the World: The Decree *Inter Mirifica*," in *Vatican II Revisited by Those Who Were There* (London: Geoffrey Chapman, 1986), 200.

3. The bibliography on analyzing the history and legacy of Vatican II is large and continues to grow. For those unfamiliar with this literature, Maureen Sullivan's *101 Questions and Answers on Vatican II* (Mahwah, NJ: Paulist Press, 2002) is a helpful basic introduction.

Council.[4] At the time of its initial reception, Ruszkowski notes, many were hoping for and would have appreciated solid doctrinal teaching on the topic of social communication.[5] Given the ongoing fluidity of the means of social communication of our present day, this doctrinal clarity remains desirable for many professional ministers. When it comes to the digital media, it is enticing to imagine a clear path ahead, with definitive answers to questions such as *"how do we understand them* and *what do we do with them?"* In 1963 Catholics wondered likewise about broadcast media, yet the final version of *Inter Mirifica* resisted too much doctrinal prescriptiveness, frustrating those who recognized the power of the media and sought to know how to approach it faithfully. The problem was, as the council fathers recognized, modern media and the instruments of social communication are a dynamic, global reality that have not yet fully taken form, either in terms of the evolution of the instruments, the way these means have shaped and continue to shape culture, or the emerging scholarship around the topic.

Aware that the means of social communication formed an emerging topic, *Inter Mirifica* thus weighed less on *how do we understand them* and significantly more so on *what do we do with them.* For this reason, the document is predominantly moral and pastoral in its wisdom, focusing on guidelines to shape the practice of communication in the Church and society. At the same time, recognizing that the overall vision of faithful communication still merited doctrinal articulation, *Inter Mirifica* also set up a generative structure for such a practical theology to emerge, as it did so in the 1971 pastoral instruction *Communio et Progressio*, the topic of the next chapter. Commentators often treat *Inter Mirifica* and *Communio et Progressio* together, honoring the pastoral instruction as a completion of the conciliar decree. Acknowledging the close association between these two documents, each of them merit a chapter in this study with a special eye toward how they edify the process of professional ministerial formation.

---

4. Andre Ruszkowski, "Decree on the Means of Social Communication: Success or Failure of the Council?," in *Vatican II Assessment and Perspectives: Twenty Five Years After (1962–1987)*, vol. 3, ed. Rene Latourelle (Mahwah, NJ: Paulist Press, 1987), 550.

5. Ibid., 549.

History and Context

The Second Vatican Council addressed the topic of social communication over two and a half days from November 23 to November 26, 1962. Compared to other discussions, this treatment was relatively brief. Before the topic of social communication was discussed, the council fathers grappled with the liturgy, then with revelation. After social communication, the topics of Christian unity, the Blessed Virgin Mary, and the Church were next on the agenda. Social communication's place on the agenda was therefore intentional: it was considered a lighter topic, and perceived as a "break" after the heavier discussions of liturgy and revelation, even termed as an "opportunity for relaxation" by Cardinal Cento, the president of the Commission for the Lay Apostolate, which housed the secretariat that prepared the schema for discussion.[6] This perception shaped the attention given to the topic itself, especially as some council fathers peeked ahead at the schema on the Blessed Virgin Mary and on the Church, both distributed at the same time as the discussion on social communication was beginning to unfold.[7] Additionally, as compared to the liturgy, revelation, and the other topics on the agenda, some council fathers wondered about whether social communication was theological enough of a topic to merit a conciliar discussion and a document. Cardinal Cento acknowledged this sentiment in his introduction to the debate. As Xavier Rynne documents, Cento "asked for the good will of the audience in dealing with a matter which though not strictly theological in substance, was still a most important element in the pastoral work of the Church."[8] In the midst of these doubts, distractions, and the desire for an easy discussion, the topic of social communication came before the council fathers.

In order to prepare the council for this discussion, a preparatory secretariat drafted a schema on the topic between 1960 and 1962. Their task was to formulate a doctrine on social communication, including guid-

---

6. Norman Tanner, *The Church and the World: Gaudium et Spes, Inter Mirifica* (Mahwah, NJ: Paulist Press, 2005), 96.

7. Xavier Rynne, *Letters from Vatican City: Vatican Council II (First Session): Background and Debates* (New York: Farrar, Strauss, and Company, 1963), 175.

8. Ibid., 176.

ance on forming the conscience for the right use of the media; emphasis on how faith and morals might shape film, radio, and television; and how these might be used to proclaim the Gospel.[9] The resulting draft spanned forty pages and included four main sections dealing with the Church's doctrine, its apostolate, Church discipline and order, and observations on particular media.[10] This document was disseminated to the council members as the discussion on revelation wrapped up on November 21, 1962. On November 24, Cardinal Cento opened the discussion on it and then gave the floor to Archbishop Stourm of Sens who outlined the schema in hand. For two and a half days, fifty-four council fathers gave brief addresses about the topic in response to the schema, while an additional forty-three respondents submitted written feedback.[11] This feedback was registered and returned to the preparatory secretariat to work on a revised draft. Between December of 1962 and June of 1963, the secretariat considered the feedback received from the council and worked on a drastic reduction of the text. A year later, in November of 1963, this revised and much shorter draft was recirculated, voted upon chapter by chapter then as a whole. It gained final approval on December 4, after which Pope Paul VI promulgated the document as the conciliar decree *Inter Mirifica*.

Studying the survey of the addresses given at Vatican II is a fascinating task. It at once reveals how inspired this gathering of the Church was, and also grounds it as an experience that was at the same time completely and fully human. The addresses offered in response to the schema on social communication ranged from the insightful to the worrisome, from the concise to the exploratory, from the constructive to the alarmist.[12] In many ways, this range of comments

9. Karlheinz Schmidthus, "Decree on the Instruments of Social Communication," in *Commentary on the Documents of Vatican II*, ed. Herbert Vorgrimler, vol. 1 (New York: Herder and Herder, 1967), 89.

10. For a more specific outline of the schema, see Tanner, *The Church and the World: Gaudium et Spes, Inter Mirifica*, 94–95.

11. Mathijs Lamberigts, "The Discussion of the Modern Media," in *History of Vatican II*, ed. Joseph A. Komonchak and Giuseppe Alberigo, vol. 2 (Maryknoll, NY: Orbis Books, 1997), 269.

12. For a summary of the main addresses articulated during this debate, see Rynne, *Letters from Vatican City: Vatican Council II (First Session): Background and Debates*, 177–85.

foreshadowed the discussions about the digital media we continue to engage in today.

While it proved to be somewhat of a struggle to maintain the council father's attention around this topic, once the discussion was under way, those who spoke generally appreciated the topic's place on the agenda and recognized its cultural and pastoral importance.[13] Initial feedback from the council members questioned the schema's length, its inward and ecclesial focus, and its overall merit as a topic for conciliar consideration.[14] Forty pages of text with a main focus on the Church missed the mark in some council fathers' assessment. Engaging in dialogue with culture around this topic and emphasizing the role of the laity in a pastoral vision forward were suggested improvements upon the existing approach of the schema.

The ongoing debate raised a variety of issues concerning the media that generally fell into two broad categories: a constructive approach that sought to explore the potential of the instruments of social communication for the Church's missionary mandate to proclaim the Gospel, and a critical approach warning against the harmful effects of the media on Church, culture, and society. In addition to these two broad categories, Kampe also points out two additional seeds planted during the discussion: exploring the Church's own use of communication, and exploring how the Church might support society's communication to promote understanding and cooperation therein.[15] In some ways, these four broad questions continue to frame the discussion around social communication in our digital culture, as the Church today considers the possibilities and risks of internet-mediated communication in and outside of the Church.

Though these larger questions animated the discussion about social communication, the draft was nonetheless approved in substance. When the revised draft returned to the council a year later in November 1963, its reception was surrounded by some tension.

---

13. For an overview of the comments, including some notable exceptions who critiqued the topic as a whole, see Lamberigts, "The Discussion of the Modern Media," 271ff.

14. Schmidthus, "Decree on the Instruments of Social Communication," 91.

15. Kampe, "Communicating with the World: The Decree" *Inter Mirifica*, 200.

Although the majority vote carried the new draft forward, there were also two minority factions that were unhappy with it to the point of starting petitions to reopen the discussion around the document. One critique challenged the vision set forth by the schema concerning the Church's relation with the press, calling it unrealistic and too prescriptive of how the two should collaborate. The other critique continued to maintain that the topic was not appropriate for an ecumenical council and that the present schema remained still too juridical and focused on the role and authority of the Church.[16] These two petitions garnered some support on the last day of the voting, but not enough to gain a majority. Still, of all the documents of Vatican II, *Inter Mirifica* remains among the ones with the largest number of negative votes in its final vote.[17] As Norman Tanner comments, dissatisfaction with the new text seems to have been widespread, but there was hesitancy around reopening the discussion on it, in lieu of moving forward:

> The council authorities were understandably reluctant in these circumstances to go back on the voting and to open up anew the whole decree. . . . Many members of the council shared these hesitations even as they became increasingly aware of both the deficiencies of the document and the importance of the topics it was treating. They did not want the council to get bogged down with the decree when it has so much else to do.[18]

Once the decree was promulgated, it received critical and often negative feedback in its reception, parallel with the concerns about it raised during the discussions of the council.[19] Reviewers were disappointed: it was considered neither an innovative nor creative document, nor one that truly explored the topic of social communication vis-à-vis the modern media. Still, the decree's value in putting the topic on the table and inviting further discussion on it was appreciated by most.

---

16. For a five-point overview of both critiques, see Schmidthus, "Decree on the Instruments of Social Communication," 92–94.
17. Eilers, *Communicating Church: Social Communication Documents*, 136.
18. Tanner, *The Church and the World: Gaudium et Spes, Inter Mirifica*, 101.
19. Ibid.

Franz-Josef Eilers notes a number of additional positive points about the legacy of *Inter Mirifica*.[20] To ensure ongoing conversation about social communication, *Inter Mirifica* established a generative structure: the commemoration of an annual World Day of Communication, a postconciliar pastoral instruction to elaborate on the topic, and a permanent institution for social communication in the Roman Curia, as well as on national and diocesan levels. In addition, as Eilers points out, *Inter Mirifica* introduced the expression "social communication" into the Church's vocabulary, a broad expression that covers "all ways, means and situations of communications in human societies."[21] This expression moved the discussion from focusing solely on the media or on the tools and instruments by which communication takes place toward the possibility of considering communication on a macro level and thus in a theological and pastoral sense as well. In this sense, the term is a bridge builder between the evolving cultural realities of communication and the wisdom of the theological tradition that is able to dialogue with it. Eilers also notes that given the increasingly social nature of digital communication today (such as the prevalence of social media and social networking), the term social communication that we inherit from Vatican II was providential for engaging in conversation with digital culture.[22]

With *Inter Mirifica*, the Church became a conversation partner to social communication. It may not have been the most exhaustive or in-depth conversation, but it opened a dialogue that continues to engage the Church and the world today. While this conciliar acknowledgement of the topic was just a silver lining for those disappointed by the document in 1963, today this conversation bears wisdom for engaging in social communication in the digital age. Ongoing dialogue with digital culture and intentional flexibility around pastoral praxis serve professional ministers much more effectively than an overly defined and prescriptive approach, which can quickly become outdated if addressing particular media. Media constantly change, and digital culture engenders a sense of user participation in the creation and sharing of information. For better or worse, a prescriptive

---

20. Eilers, *Communicating Church: Social Communication Documents*, 136–38.
21. Ibid., 136.
22. Ibid., 138.

approach for social communication today would face and clash with these cultural realities and expectations. A dialogical approach, on the other hand, allows the Church to continue to explore and assess new media for their gifts and limitations, even as these new media change.

A dialogical approach to social communication benefits the Church's fundamental task of evangelization, as the digital culture continues to provide new methods and expressions for proclaiming the Good News. At the same time, the Church's missionary mandate calls into consideration not only the means by which the message of the Gospel is communicated but also the content of the message itself and the Church's responsibility to teach it.[23] As such, dialogue also brings content: wisdom to be shared about communication for the good of culture, society, and humankind. In this regard, *Inter Mirifica* offers some key entry points that bring the tradition into intentional conversation with the cultural realities of social communication.

Overview of *Inter Mirifica*[24]

Inter Mirifica divides into four brief sections: an introduction (1–2), a chapter on doctrinal foundations (3–12), a chapter on pastoral implications (13–22), and a conclusion (23–24). The introduction sets a constructive and positive tone, referring to the "genius of humankind that has produced marvelous technical inventions from creation with God's help," and affirms the Church's interest in this.[25] At the same time, the tone is not overly optimistic: the introduction also alludes to the dangers of social communication; for example, the ways it can be "damaging or contrary to the Creator's design."[26] For this reason, the Church enters into conversation with the topic of social communication, looking to offer wisdom and guidance toward "the salvation of Christians and the progress of humankind."[27]

---

23. See Paul VI, *Evangelii Nuntiandi*.

24. Rather than a full summary, the section here is offered as a complement to the document, meant to enrich the reading of the conciliar decree.

25. See IM 1 in the translation provided by Austin Flannery, ed., *Vatican Council II: The Basic Sixteen Documents* (Northport, NY: Costello, 1996), 539.

26. IM 2.

27. Ibid.

The doctrinal foundations of *Inter Mirifica* briefly situate the Church's interest in the topic of social communication in the Church's mandate to proclaim the Gospel. It affirms that the media can contribute to the formation of the faithful and the broader pastoral work of the Church, and within an ecclesial context, it places the responsibility on the pastoral leaders of the Church to guide and show the way how. By contrast, when it comes to the broader cultural reality of the media, the document specifically names the lay faithful as those responsible to "animate the media with a Christian and human spirit."[28] As such, the scope of the document is already wide, encompassing the communication of the Church, as well as the Church's observation about the greater cultural realities of communication. The remainder of the doctrinal foundations are practical: they reinstate the Church's ethical principles on the moral order, the formation of conscience, the common good, justice, and freedom, especially as all of these pertain to the creation, sharing, access to, and dissemination of information through the instruments of social communication. If one is searching for a theology of communication among these doctrinal principles, it is not yet here. Rather, *Inter Mirifica* summarizes the ethical principles of the tradition vis-à-vis a new cultural context. By and large, the principles are directed toward greater society and the use of the media by those who authorize, produce, and receive it.

In chapter 2 of *Inter Mirifica*, the document returns to addressing the Church's own use of social communication. True to the tone of the introduction, the tone here is likewise one of tempered enthusiasm: on the one hand, the document calls all members of the Church to ensure that "the media are utilized in the service of the many works of the apostolate without delay and as energetically as possible." On the other hand, it also calls for the forestallment of any projects likely to prove harmful.[29] The responsibility is on pastoral leaders, but lay faithful who work in the media are also called to bear witness to Christ in their particular roles, as well as in collaboration with the pastoral activity of the Church.[30] Along these lines, the document envisions a wholesome Catholic press, wholesome cinematic entertainment,

28. Ibid., 3.
29. Ibid., 13.
30. Ibid.

and decent radio and television programs, as well as the intentional support of Catholic broadcasting stations.[31] The chapter reiterates that priests, religious, and laity should all receive training to actualize this vision. Laypeople in the media ought to receive appropriate Christian formation in the Church's social teaching so as to be able to witness to their faith authentically through their professional roles. Likewise, teachings on the theoretical and practical use of the media should be on the curriculum of Catholic schools, especially as they relate to principles of Christian morality and social thought. The chapter closes with a strong encouragement of ongoing support to maintain and assist the Catholic media, as well as calling for an annual day of social communication in each diocese, the creation of a pontifical office, as well as the establishment of national and diocesan structures to promote the Church's effective use of social communication.

Inter Mirifica concludes by calling for a pastoral instruction "to ensure that all the principles and rules of the council on the media may be put into effect."[32] Its final thought is an exhortation to the daughters and sons of the Church as well as all people of good will to seek only the edifying use of the media for the good of humanity, so that the name of the Lord may be glorified through them.[33] A brief but important allusion here connects the media of social communication to other media in the history of the Church, namely, the great masterworks of art that served the Church's evangelizing mission from its beginnings.

Assessing the document as a whole, we may summarize its key points as follows:

- Its tone is one of tempered enthusiasm, clearly urging and promoting the use of the media, while at the same time warning of its dangers.
- It roots the Church's interest in social communication in the Church's own missionary mandate and in the tradition of other media in the past used for this purpose.

---

31. Ibid., 14.
32. Ibid., 23.
33. Ibid., 24.

- Its vision is threefold: the Church's own use of the media for the apostolate, the Catholic media in service of the Church, and the function of lay faithful imbuing the secular media with a Christian and human spirit.
- Its doctrinal foundations rest on the moral and ethical principles of Catholic social thought.
- It encourages training and formation in the media for priests, religious, and all the faithful. The initiative within the Church is with the pastoral leadership, while in the secular media, it rests with lay Christian media professionals.
- It communicates ongoing commitment to this topic, with the call for a pastoral instruction, an annual day, a pontifical office, and national and diocesan structures.

Forming Ministers

As ministerial formation toward effective engagement with the media is of special interest to this study, *Inter Mirifica*'s vision for formation merits examination. Even though *Inter Mirifica* is among the briefest of documents of Vatican II, its scope is broad, encompassing the Church, the Catholic media, and the secular media, and all the respective roles of lay, religious, and ordained therein. Because of this broad scope, the document did not get too specific about formation, other than the fact that it is necessary, either in terms of media literacy or Catholic social teaching (the latter reflecting the moral and ethical principles the document presents as doctrinal foundations). Along these lines, *Inter Mirifica* mentions formation on several occasions.

In its first chapter, the document notes that the media themselves are of formative value to the Christian faithful. Christians are called to follow the guidance of pastoral leaders in their use and interpretation. The document asserts the importance of the formation of conscience regarding the media and moral and ethical matters. It highlights the need for access to and dissemination of information toward the common good, the right to information and its authenticity, the preservation of human dignity in communication, the right of artful expression toward the moral order, and the need for an edifying rather than harmful representation of evil. The document urges moderation and discipline vis-à-vis media consumption, and invites the practice of discernment to fully understand the content of the message that reaches one as audience.

To sum up, the concept of formation regarding social communication entails a twofold responsibility: the responsibility of pastoral leaders to help the people they serve access and interpret the media, and the responsibility of all communicators and receivers to form the conscience toward ethically sound communication practices. For pastoral leaders and ministerial professionals, this twofold emphasis in fact is one, as enabling the formation of conscience is part and parcel of ministry, especially in teaching, pastoral counseling, and spiritual direction. To serve accordingly then, pastoral leaders themselves need formation in understanding the media and understanding the moral issues that they highlight in a particular way.

Along these lines, the second chapter of *Inter Mirifica* highlights the formative potential of the Catholic press and other forms of mass media, including theater. It follows this overview of Catholic media with the assertion that "priests, religious and laity should be trained at once to meet the needs described above."[34] While this directive may seem a bit all encompassing, the focus here is both on media literacy and firm rootedness in Catholic moral tradition so as to make wise and life-giving choices through engagement with them. Following from this, the document outlines technical, doctrinal, and moral formation for lay media professionals, as well as formation suited to both the specific medium and the needs of specific groups exploring its use. The chapter reemphasizes the importance of moral formation in Catholic educational institutions with an eye toward social communication, as well as a clear and concise summary of relevant doctrine in the Catechism.

Putting these references to formation in dialogue with the comprehensive fourfold vision of ministerial formation of *Optatam Totius*, *Pastores Dabo Vobis*, and the national documents thereafter, one can clearly discern certain aspects of intellectual, human, spiritual, and pastoral formation in *Inter Mirifica*. *Inter Mirifica*'s emphasis on the formation of conscience and rootedness in the Catholic moral tradition encompasses the intellectual understanding of the tradition; the

34. Ibid., 15.

spiritual openness to abide by it; the human sensitivity to respect basic rights, dignity, and the common good; and the pastoral skill to live as a particular community in a specific cultural context. However, the challenge of gaining media literacy as part of formation spans all four of these categories.

Media literacy assumes the ability to accurately and effectively interpret a particular medium and the skill set to successfully communicate and/or receive communication with this medium's help. Media literacy also implies a thorough understanding of one's cultural context, as well as the skill to communicate within this context toward mutual and communal understanding. Taking radio broadcasting as an example, literacy for this medium on the part of the broadcaster takes into account the basic skill set to work comfortably in a studio or with particular equipment, the understanding of nonvisual communication, and the necessary verbal skills to broadcast well, as well as relevant assumptions about audience, such as where the broadcast is heard and what people are likely doing while listening to it (commuting, working, engaging in leisure activities). On the part of the listener, media literacy for the radio involves the skill set to operate a radio and the ability to interpret audio communication that may be live, prerecorded, interactive, or one-way. Awareness of audience also plays a part of the listener's media literacy, as it is significant for interpretation whether a broadcast is on a local, national, or international level.

Formation or training for such comprehensive literacy involves fostering both skills and understanding. Undoubtedly it is important for media literacy to gain the basic technical skills to access particular media or, if needed, to participate in their production. For this type of training, ministry formation need not reinvent the wheel, but may instead fruitfully collaborate with professionals who work and serve in these fields. Gaining understanding of the media and helping others interpret and interact with them in the light of faith, on the other hand, is a growth process that is well situated within the context of ministerial formation. This type of formation calls on a combination of the four areas outlined in the pastoral formation documents of *Optatam Totius* and thereafter.

Media literacy toward understanding implies intellectual formation so that a minister can recognize how communication patterns via a particular medium may conceal or reveal the truth of the content of faith. The theological foundations of communication itself become important here, as will be fleshed out in the analysis of the pastoral instruction *Communio et Progressio*. For *Inter Mirifica*, the content of faith in focus is the moral wisdom of the tradition, and as such, a suitable intellectual formation toward media literacy invites ministers into the depth of this wisdom so as to be able to identify moral issues and ethical challenges when it comes to a particular medium.

Media literacy toward understanding necessarily assumes human formation. As noted in the introduction, human formation fosters the minister's ability to relate to others, an essential skill in facilitating encounter with Jesus Christ. Human formation is a salient area when it comes to media, as media are rooted in communication—an essentially relational activity. This aspect of ministerial formation thus considers the media and asks what potential they carry for moving participants from communication toward community and ultimately communion. In the Christian tradition, God's self-communication is expressed relationally: in the *person* of Jesus Christ, who is both its mediator and its fullness.[35] As such, the ability to assess media by the standard of how it allows people to form authentic and life-giving relationships is essential to an overall media literacy for ministry. In *Inter Mirifica*, the ongoing emphasis on moral and ethical principles for social communication is ultimately rooted in this principle: how to relate well with one another in a way that is faithful to the example of Christ.

Closely related to human formation is spiritual formation, which moves human relationality into the realm of human-divine relationality. This aspect of formation intersects with media literacy insofar as it helps to bring about discernment regarding how particular media can serve the human search for God and how they enhance or create a context for prayer. For anyone who has been moved by a religious film or by an international broadcast such as Pope Francis's first appearance on the balcony on the night of his election, this potential is clear. The challenge of this aspect of media literacy is where the spiritual message is more subtle or not named in explicitly Christian terms. Ministerial professionals are called here to help others inter-

35. *Dei Verbum*, 2.

pret the message and discern how it illuminates, dialogues with, or hinders the spiritual path of the Christian. If Marshall McLuhan's now-classic adage that "the medium is the message" is correct, then the medium itself that communicates the message also shapes the spiritual potential it carries. Interestingly, the coining of this phrase was contemporary with the publication of *Inter Mirifica*.[36]

Pastoral formation intersects with media literacy significantly, especially when it comes to fostering understanding in the community and for the good of the community. The pastoral aspect of ministerial formation leads to a commitment to ministry in context: its goal is to enable ministers to live out their intellectual, human, and spiritual gifts in a specific cultural and professional setting. Awareness of creation, culture, and the dynamics of social structures, systems, and institutions is essential for this so that the Gospel message may be proclaimed and lived in the most relevant way and in a fashion that people can resonate with it here and now. In a similar fashion, media literacy for understanding is deeply contextual. There is no such thing as a generic communication: language itself already embeds communication in a cultural context. Helping people interpret a particular medium is facilitating awareness of the contextual dynamics of the message that reaches them and how the Christian tradition dialogues with this overall act of communication. For example, the 2004 film *The Passion of the Christ* was well attended in audience and thus generated ample discussion in a variety of cultural, ecclesial, and academic contexts. Part of these discussions was pastoral media literacy in action: highlighting the role of the spirituality of Mel Gibson, the film's writer and director; highlighting a major thematic inspiration behind the film, the medieval tradition of contemplating the passion; and highlighting the similarities and differences between an artistic interpretation of the passion on film and the lived ecclesial, liturgical, and biblical understanding of these events as cherished by Christian communities are just a few examples of how conversations around *The Passion of the Christ* connected context, media literacy, and theology. Media literacy formation for pastoral leaders anticipates conversations like this and empowers ministers to be able to identify

36. Marshall McLuhan, *Understanding the Media: The Extensions of Man* (New York: Mentor, 1964).

and invite people into these connections. All this is closely related to what *Inter Mirifica* identifies as the pastoral task: the preaching of the Gospel and the work of the apostolate.[37]

Legacy for Digital Ministry Formation: We Are All Communicators

In 1963, the world of social communication implied distinct points within the flow of information: communicators who produced and shared information and a mass audience who received it. Communicators (whether journalists, actors, broadcasting professionals, as well as all those who produced the information shared by these) had great power and perceived authority to shape public opinion and even to identify truth. *Inter Mirifica* recognizes this as it states: "Public opinion exercises enormous influence nowadays over the lives, private or public, of all citizens, of whatever class. It is therefore necessary that all members of society meet the demands of justice and charity in this domain and that they try, through the media, to form and expand sound public opinion."[38]

While *Inter Mirifica* is an accurate reflection of its day in assuming a difference and interaction between distinct communicators and receivers, it is prophetic in the above-quoted passage. In calling all members of society to honor justice and charity in the forming of public opinion, *Inter Mirifica* speaks in the most relevant terms to digital culture.

Internet-mediated communication, especially after the advent of Web 2.0 technologies and beyond, has shifted the paradigm of social or mass communication. Instead of clear roles differentiating senders and receivers of information, social communication in the digital age implies simultaneous roles of sending *and* receiving information, as well as the increasing and parallel role of producing it. Rather than one to many, the social communication schema of the digital age is many to many. Traditional communicators of perceived authority, such as journalists, broadcasters, and other media professionals, are

37. IM 13–15.
38. Ibid., 8.

still part of this interconnected network, but their voices are joined and rounded out by the comments, feedback, and original contributions of the audience, giving the audience a newfound power to generate attention around particular information. In the digital age, we have all become communicators, with access to the technological skills and the flow of information online. As such, the standards of justice and charity do indeed befall on all members of society, not just on those who are media professionals who normally operate under a code of ethical standards in their work. In a digital culture, if all members of society have some access to shaping public opinion, and yet only the communications professionals abide by certain ethical code to do so, an urgency arises around preserving human dignity and the common good. Cyberbullying and all of its tragic consequences is but one alarming example of why this urgency is relevant and important to consider.

Ministerial formation in the digital age has to take this shared role of communication into account. As traditional voices of authority in media culture have been integrated into a greater choir (or sometimes cacophony) of voices, the ecclesial voice of authority also realizes that it is not alone in speaking about faith in the digital age. Pastoral leaders whom *Inter Mirifica* charged with guiding the faithful about the ethical and fruitful use of the media are now charged with enabling the whole Church, not just as audience, but as faithful communicators who are likely contributing to public opinion, whether on a blog, a social networking profile, or simply through their comments and passing on of information. Faithful interpretation of the media is no longer just about how to make sense of what we receive; it is formation for all to discern regarding how to faithfully take part in and contribute to the flow of information. Offering a voice to all, this participatory digital culture engenders a powerful opportunity to empower all the baptized to take part in their ecclesial mission to evangelize and thus connect with others and share the Good News on an unprecedented scale.

At the same time, this new participatory culture comes with particular challenges, especially those of discerning information as authentic and true. Just as media professionals abide by an ethical code of conduct in their work, the ecclesial voice of the pastoral leader also speaks out of a magisterial structure that frames the content of faith. This ecclesial structure authenticates the professional voice of the pastoral leader who serves the Word that has been revealed and handed on as the content of faith. But in this digital culture in which we have all become communicators, serious questions arise. What structures are in place to help frame the public voice of faith of the Catholic mom who reflects on her blog about faith and family; the college student who builds his social networking profile around how he is drawn to radical social thought; or the traditionalist who feels passionately about pre–Vatican II liturgy and shares this through regular multimedia uploads? What is the standard by which these different expressions of faith are called to shape the public opinion about the Catholic tradition? Differences in understanding the tradition have existed since the inception of the Church. What has changed with the digital age is that these diverse voices can all become public and even authoritative to some degree.

How can pastoral leaders offer guidance in this shifting context? To simply filter online voices that shape public opinion but do not necessarily abide by an ecclesial or magisterial interpretation of the content of faith does not seem a feasible solution, nor one that has been pursued by the Church: for example, the moderators of the papal twitter account @Pontifex seem intentional in their decision not to filter or block comments that are negative, contrary, or even offensive. Instead, one way the pastoral leader can serve a community is through fostering media literacy that is imbued with an understanding of the tradition so as to enable the community to discern and dialogue with a variety of perspectives mushrooming online. The challenge of coming across digital content and wondering about its source is an experience that most people who have sought information online share. Offering guidance on how to determine any given online source as authentic and true to the content of faith is one aspect of communal formation that is highly relevant for faith in the digital culture. This is also a salient new area for adult faith formation, one that lies outside of the traditional sacramental preparation context.

In addition to simply filtering out content, what also seems unfeasible in a digital culture—one in which we are all communicators—is for a single pastoral leader to bear the responsibility for understanding faith, culture, and the media and interpreting this for a community of people. While pastoral leadership is often a demanding role of service, bearing the sole responsibility for faithful digital media awareness is an undue pressure on individual priests or lay ministers. Given that digital culture is defined by participation, collaboration, and sharing in the public forum, pastoral leadership that approaches digital media literacy as a shared effort may well be a more viable path. Creating an advisory or consultative team that includes the pastoral leader, as well as those who are comfortable with a variety of media and those who minister to key populations within the community, can together bring the theological, technical, and sociocultural expertise of the entire community to the pastoral issues surrounding the digital media. Such a collaborative structure is in line with the vision of Vatican II and the specific recommendations of *Inter Mirifica* that called for curial, national, and diocesan units to focus on social communication. Creating a digital media ministry team follows this line of structuring, whether at the parish level or a similarly local level such as campus ministry, an educational institution, a health-care facility, a spiritual formation facility, or a faith-based service organization.

Envisioning engagement with the digital media as a team effort is a rich inheritance from *Inter Mirfica* for ministerial formation today. One premise of this study is that the constant evolution of new media both thrills and fascinates, but it can also overwhelm and intimidate those who are endeavoring to keep up with it. Pooling wisdom, skill, expertise, and human resources alleviates pressure while also making space for creativity to emerge in the process of discerning how a community's digital presence can serve the apostolate. Likewise, an advisory or consultative team working in concert with a pastoral leader conveys an integral reality of digital culture: many voices matter. Following from this, the pastoral leader's task of guiding people to be faithful communicators themselves resonates more authentically with the participatory cultural reality of our digital age. It is guidance emerging out of communal wisdom toward communal witness of the Good News.

2 TOWARD A THEOLOGY OF COMMUNICATION

Communio et Progressio: Pastoral Instruction on the Means of Social Communication (1971)

After the promulgation of *Inter Mirifica* in 1963, both its critics and its supporters were well aware that the document did not exhaust all that could be said on the topic of social communication and all that this topic implied for the mission, activity, and witness of the Church. *Inter Mirifica* itself articulated an invitation to further conversation, as it stated in its conclusion that the newly envisioned office of the Holy See, which in 1964 came to be the Pontifical Commission for Social Communication, should publish a pastoral instruction "to ensure that all principles and rules of the council on the media be put into effect."[1] From 1964 to 1971, this commission focused on this task to produce the document *Communio et Progressio*.

On the twenty-fifth anniversary of the Second Vatican Council, Cardinal Andrzej Deskur, president emeritus of the Pontifical Commission for Social Communications, reflected back on the significance of the council's work on the topic of social communication.[2] He

1. *Inter Mirifica*, 32.
2. Andrzej Deskur, "Twentieth Anniversary of *Communio et Progressio*: Post-Conciliar Instruction seen as Last Council Document," *L'Osservatore Romano* (English) 1180 (March 4, 1991), 2.

considered *Communio et Progressio* so closely aligned with the work of the council that it could be regarded as Vatican II's last document. As Deskur reflected, the name of the document, "communion and progress," sums up the vision and legacy of the council itself, evoking the sense of dialogue, unity, and aggiornamento in the Church's posture toward the world.

As compared to *Inter Mirifica, Communio et Progressio* is a maturation of the Church's thought on the topic of social communication. During the council, *Inter Mirifica*'s early place on the agenda prevented it from benefiting from the council's most profound work; it was discussed during the first session preceding work on key documents such as *Lumen Gentium* and *Gaudium et Spes. Communio et Progressio*, on the other hand, had the benefit of gleaning from the emerging conciliar wisdom of the Church, and it acknowledges especially drawing from *Gaudium et Spes, Unitatis Redintegratio, Dignitatis Humanae, Ad Gentes Divinitus, Christus Dominus,* as well as *Inter Mirifica.*[3] Because of this broader scope, the document moved beyond simply an implementation of the principles and rules of the council on the media, as per the original directive of *Inter Mirifica.* Instead, *Communio et Progressio* elaborated on both the theological foundations and practical, ethical implications of communicating the Good News as Church. As Andre Ruszkowski notes, this elaboration received some criticism as a departure from *Inter Mirifica* by the introduction of topics not strictly found in the conciliar decree.[4] However, among these new topics was an articulation of a theology of communication.

More elaborate in its theological foundations than *Inter Mirifica*— it introduced a more intentional emphasis on theology proper to communication—*Communio et Progressio* left an invaluable inheritance for practical theology and the practice of ministry with and for social communication. This inheritance guides ministers and pastoral leaders back into an ever-more profound understanding

---

3. *Communio et Progressio,* 2.

4. Andre Ruszkowski, "The Decree on the Means of Social Communication: Success or Failure of the Council?," in *Vatican II Assessment and Perspectives Twenty-Five Years After (1962–1987),* ed. Rene Latourelle (Mahwah, NJ: Paulist Press, 1989), 555.

of the topic of social communication, even as the particular media might change. In 1963, when the council fathers reflected on social communication, they made the decision that laying out a full theological understanding of the media was less within the scope of *Inter Mirifica* than was envisioning faithful practical and ethical praxis for Church, culture, and society. Yet in order to continue engaging in practical theology and ministry, and in the cycle of faithful action and reflection that animates the ministerial task, some further conceptual foundations were necessary. In articulating a theology of communication, *Communio et Progressio* provided this conceptual foundation for social communication, steadily bringing theology into the ongoing conversation in a way that has proven fruitful even while particular media continue to change over time. After an overview of the history, context, and key points of *Communio et Progressio*, this chapter returns to its theological legacy as we explore what it holds for ministerial formation in the digital age.

History and Context

On January 21, 1971, Pope Paul VI expressed his support for the final draft of *Communio et Progressio* in a letter addressed to the president of the Pontifical Commission for Social Communication, Archbishop John Martin O'Connor. In this letter, the pope calls the preparation process that got the document to that point "long, laborious and diligent."[5] Indeed, the commission and its consultants worked for seven years, generating five entirely new drafts during this time. Similar to the genesis of the conciliar documents, the preparation for the pastoral instruction began with a global questionnaire, disseminated to bishops and their communications committees worldwide in the beginning of 1965. Gathering the responses, the commission formulated a set of directives as a starting point for their work. With the help of forty international consultants, the commission gathered and regathered multiple times between 1966 and 1970 to synthesize the work, generating five substantively different

---

5. Deskur, "Twentieth Anniversary of *Communio et Progressio*," 2.

drafts, each under the guidance of distinct people.[6] The document was finalized after January of 1971 when the pope articulated his support through the letter noted above. Subsequently, the finished document was published and promulgated on May 24, 1971.

Key Points

From its beginning, *Communio et Progessio* echoes the conciliar spirit as it invites dialogue by addressing both the Church and the greater culture. It approaches the topic of social communication from three related angles: theology, culture, and ecclesial practice. The first part of the document, "The Christian View of the Means of Social Communication: Basic Points of Doctrine" (paragraphs 6–18) lays out the theological foundations of communication most relevant for the topic at hand and will be addressed in detail below. The next section, "The Contribution of the Communications Media to Human Progress," continues the practical-moral trajectory of *Inter Mirifica* by revisiting its key points about human communication. Within the theme of human communication, *Communio et Progressio* focuses especially on public opinion (24–32), the right and access to information (33–43), and the freedom of communication (44–47) in greater detail. This section also introduces more elaborate emphasis on education and entertainment (48–53), artistic expression (54–58), advertising (59–62), fostering training and media literacy for all (64–72), opportunities and obligations for communicators and recipients (73–83), and the virtues of collaboration between citizens, civil authorities, nations, Christians, and all people of faith (84–100), all as particular aspects of human communication. After these broad strokes, the third section of the document brings the discussion home to the Catholic ecclesial context, envisioning social communication in and by the Church.

Implicit in the very structure of the document is a dialogical approach between theology, culture, and the practice of the Church. It is significant that the practical-moral analysis of human communication precedes the section on the Church's own communication, implying

---

6. Jacques Cousineau, *L'Eglise et Mass Media*, vol. 16 (Montreal, Canada: Office des Communications Sociales, 1973). For a detailed description of the preparatory process and persons involved with each draft, see chapter 6.

that the human communication practices envisioned in part 2 of the document bear wisdom for the activity of the Church as well. We see this most clearly as part 3 reiterates the importance of dialogue and freedom of public opinion within the Church and as observed by the Church (114–124).[7] Part 3 also delves into the practical implications of the theology presented in part 1 for the life of the Church, as it considers the Church's communication practices, as well as particular media for this essential task of communication: print, film, radio, television, and theater (125–160). The document concludes by enumerating a number of pastoral directives for the work of the Church concerning the institutional structuring and training for effective social communication as part of the Church' evangelizing task (161–178). The parting thought of *Communio et Progressio* echoes the dynamism of the topic of social communication, asserts the importance of ongoing dialogue, praxis, and reflection, as the "people of God continue to walk in history" (185).

Training and Formation

As training and formation are a special focus of this study, *Communio et Progressio*'s treatment of these also deserves mention. Largely, these topics are found in the second chapter of part 2 and the first chapter of part 3, with occasional references elsewhere.[8] These two main sections on the topic approach it with distinct but related lenses. Part 2 approaches training as a media literacy, a skilled understanding of social communication in a particular sociocultural context. As the document describes this: "training should include a practical consideration of the special nature of each medium and of its status in the local community and how it can best be utilized, and this should be done with special reference to man and society."[9] *Communio et Progressio* envisions such a base competency in media literacy for all; it is a skill for communication and thus participation in society. For

7. As noted by Paul A. Soukup, "Church Documents and the Media," in *Mass Media*, ed. John Coleman and Miklos Tomka, vol. 6 (London: SCM Press, 1993), 73ff.

8. Training is treated in part 2, chapter 2, paragraphs 64–72; part 3, chapter 1, paragraphs 106–111, as well as in paragraphs 164, 170. Formation is noted in paragraph 141.

9. CP 64.

"recipients of the media," this base competency implies the sensitivity to be able to interpret a particular medium effectively, discerning whether its message is one "based on sound morality," a foundation that assumes right relationship with God and mercy and justice among humankind.[10] For "communicators" or media professionals, the document also envisions skill, sound knowledge, and experience to be able to carry out their work. As with the virtue of sound morality for the recipients of media, *Communio et Progressio* similarly emphasizes the importance of human qualities in the training of the professional communicator. Here the document is demonstrating practical application of its earlier articulated theological foundations of communication, especially echoing the act of Christ's perfect communication as "a giving of self in love."[11] In this light, *Communio et Progressio* reminds media professionals that their service to human communication is one that, fundamentally, is an activity to connect and unite humankind. To do this well, one must know and love others. Paragraph 73 thus articulates this for media professionals:

> Communicators breathe life into the dialogue that happens within the family of man. It is they who preside while the exchange proceeds around the vast "round table" that the media have made. Their vocation is nobly to promote the purpose of social communication. This purpose is to accelerate every sort of human progress and to increase cooperation among men until there exists a genuine communion among them.

This trajectory from connection to communion is essential to the theology of communication of this document and is reflected in its practical, professional vision for people who work in the media. In their training and formation for their task, the centrality of the human person in his and her essential relationality cannot be overshadowed by technical skill, competition to be relevant, or the desire to consistently offer the latest information first. The practical-moral vision of what makes for good social communication also rests on this essential question of how a medium enables people to move from connection

10. Ibid., 67.
11. See ibid., 6–18, especially paragraph 11, as well as the section of this chapter on the theology of communication below.

to communion. As such, both for professional communicators and the people who receive the message, the ultimate hope of people in communion cannot be lost. Communicators must consistently work toward a vision of "making the process of communication a communion of the spirit."[12]

In addition to envisioning media literacy and media competency that maintains the human person at the center, *Communio et Progressio* also teaches briefly on formation and training specifically for pastoral leaders and ministers. By and large, *Communio et Progressio* echoes *Inter Mirifica* here in asserting that media literacy and competency are part and parcel of ministerial formation and merit support from both educational institutions and the local and national ecclesial infrastructure. Along these lines, as *Communio et Progressio* stresses that "media literacy is necessary to take part in modern life and to be at all effective in the apostolate," it also recommends that "knowledge about how the media work upon the fabric of society and the technique of their use" ought to play a part in formation curricula.[13] Likewise and parallel to this, national and diocesan offices are called to foster the ongoing media literacy of lay and clerical faithful by the means of courses, conferences, study sessions, and other forms of continuing education opportunities.[14] Recalling the fourfold approach to comprehensive ministerial formation that incorporates the intellectual, human, spiritual, and pastoral competencies, *Communio et Progressio*'s reiteration of the importance of formation resonates therein. Media literacy—in the broad vision of the document—consistently assumes communicators who understand the centrality of the human person situated in his or her cultural context and embedded in a network of relationships. The theological vision of the document helps to situate this understanding within a Christology that reveals the sharing of self in love as a theological, moral, and pastoral standard. As a minister in formation gains media literacy, these sociocultural, theological, moral, and pastoral understandings necessarily accompany the gaining of technical skill for the apostolate.

In summary, as compared to *Inter Mirifica*, *Communio et Progressio* benefitted from time, a better sense of the council's overall work and

12. Ibid., 72.
13. Ibid., 111.
14. Ibid., 169.

vision, the sustained seven-year collaboration of experts from around the world, and the example of *Inter Mirifica*'s own genesis, including the tensions and critiques that surrounded its final promulgation. The combination of these resulted in a document that aimed to continue the conversation. As per its charge, *Communio et Progressio* picked up on the points initiated in *Inter Mirifica* and elaborated on them, following the practical-moral and pastoral approaches defining the conciliar document. In addition to following these threads to greater detail, the experience of the council and the benefit of time also allowed for the introduction of a more articulate theological foundation and a more intentional structure in the approach of the document. Paul Soukup makes a fair observation that the social communication documents of the Church try to do too much with limited methods of analysis and confusing approaches; this rings true of *Communio et Progressio*, especially in terms of all that it strives to accomplish in scope.[15] The threefold approach to the topic is, however, more clear and systematic than was the much-condensed and edited final version of *Inter Mirifica*. Thus it is a workable foundation for dialogue and praxis. If beginning the conversation was the hallmark phrase of *Inter Mirifica*, then ongoing dialogue encapsulates the spirit of *Communio et Progressio*. Aware of both its task and its limitations regarding the fluid topic of the media, the pastoral instruction engages in dialogue in ways that are both implicit in its structure and explicit in its content. Human communication and its various cultural elements are partners in the conversation, a conversation to which the Church brings theological and moral wisdom. But the Church also seeks to learn from it for her own pastoral and evangelizing task. Wisely, the pastoral instruction envisions this dialogue as ongoing, rooted in a theology that moves humankind from connection to communion.

A Theology of Communication

In C. S. Lewis's *The Great Divorce*, we encounter an image of hell that touches eerily on our contemporary experience. Departing from the traditional image of hell as fiery torment set in a cavernous, under-

15. Soukup, "Church Documents and the Media," 71.

ground place populated by devils, *The Great Divorce* instead presents us with a vast and ever-growing city, shrouded in rainy half-light, where the gloomy and quarrelsome inhabitants continue to move farther and farther away from each other. As one of the more seasoned inhabitants describes the place to another: "There is a bit of rising ground near where I live and a chap has a telescope. You can see the lights of the inhabited houses, where those old ones live, millions of miles away. Millions of miles from us and from one another. Every now and then they move further still."[16] This image of hell is rooted in utter isolation—from God, self, and one another. The inhabitants of hell turn so inward that they lose the sense of life-giving relationality central to the *imago Dei*. The ever-growing city is a symbol of the human person's self-imposed torment in willful isolation.

If utter isolation evokes for us the torment of hell, then relationship, community, and communion invite us into the mystery of God's eternal salvation. For this reason, *Communio et Progressio* begins its theological articulation of communication by affirming the potential of human contact as a starting point on the trajectory from connection to communication to community to communion. The document approaches social communication and its technological instruments in a constructive light, noting that "these technical advances have the high purpose of bringing people together into closer contact with one another."[17] Understanding the theology of the next twelve paragraphs of *Communio et Progressio* hinges on understanding the movement from connection to communion and the wisdom of the tradition that sheds particular light on this trajectory. As the document affirms: "A Christian estimate of the contribution that the media make to the well-being of humankind is rooted in this fundamental principle."[18] Rooted in affirming the potential of human connection, the document relies on three key theological concepts to move this connection toward communion: creativity, Trinity, and the image of Christ as Perfect Communicator.

16. C. S. Lewis, *The Great Divorce* (San Francisco: Harper Collins Edition, 2001), 11.
17. CP 6.
18. Ibid.

Creativity

Fundamentally, what animates the movement on the trajectory from connection to communion is the creative human spirit in cooperation with God. Human creativity is the human person's capacity to be inventive and generative. It is a unique and essential attribute of our nature. From the perspective of Catholic theology, this attribute is rooted in the *imago Dei*, in the human person's ontology in the image and likeness of God (Gen 1:27). God is the original Creator and ultimate Giver of Life. The human person, in his and her creativity, always points back to the Creator and manifests this causal connection between divine and human nature. *Communio et Progressio* relies on *Gaudium et Spes* to articulate this foundation, citing a section of the conciliar constitution that offers a theology of human activity that highlights even our daily work as the "prolongation of the work of the creator, a service to other men and women, and a personal contribution to the fulfillment in history of the divine plan."[19] Viewed in this light, technological advances in communication as expressions of human creativity have tremendous potential for the good of humankind. If emerging out of God-given creativity, then the means of social communication are truly instruments of community and communion. Consistent with the constructive and visionary spirit of Vatican II, *Communio et Progressio* offers the following as an inspiring vision of what the fullness of social communication could be in the divine plan for human life and society. Paragraph 7 asserts:

> It is within this vision that the means of social communication thus fall into their proper place. They help men share their knowledge and unify their creative work. Indeed by creating man in His own image, God has given him a share in his creative power. And so man is summoned to cooperate with his fellow man in building the earthly city.[20]

Technological innovation as an expression of God-given creativity frames social communication within the divine plan and invites humankind into it as coparticipants through our generativity. This vision of human creativity is highly constructive and seeks to inspire. Aware

---

19. *Gaudium et Spes*, 34.
20. CP 7.

that human genius can also be used for evil, this inspiring vision intentionally connects human creativity with the Creator and yields an implicit standard: human creativity in the image of the Creator is one that is necessarily life-giving for humankind.

Trinity

Rooted in the *imago Dei*, the theology of human creativity invites us back to the Creator, who is not only life-giving but also the very foundation of community and communion. The trinitarian God as the communion of Father, Son, and Spirit is both the source and fulfillment of human communion and thus serves as the fundamental theological standard of social communication. As *Communio et Progressio* states:

> In the Christian faith, the unity and brotherhood of man are the chief aims of all communication and these find their source and model in the central mystery of the eternal communion between the Father, Son and Holy Spirit who live a single divine life.[21]

Trinitarian theology as the foundation of social communication may seem like an impossible combination of the all-encompassing mystery with the utterly practical. Very often, our pastoral encounters with trinitarian theology come with a ubiquitous warning not to get too near, as it is all a mystery and thus impossible to understand. This stereotype pushes the Trinity to the margins of our practical theology and spirituality and inadvertently uproots who we are and what we do as Christians from our most basic foundation—the very nature of God. While it is true that God's trinitarian nature is beyond our full understanding, the concept of mystery here is one that beckons us with invitation rather than halting us like a stop sign. Veiled in mystery, our trinitarian God calls us to come ever nearer until we may see God face-to-face in eternal life (1 Cor 13:12). The mystery is the gradual unfolding of our understanding, experience, and relationship with God.

21. Ibid., 8.

Given this invitation into the mystery of the Trinity, how does God's nature illuminate our social communication practices as Church and society? By considering God's being as communication and communion between Father, Son, and Spirit, we have a theological vision to contextualize our practices. Bernard Haring makes this connection explicit as he explores the trinitarian dimensions of communication:

> Jesus, the Word incarnate, reveals the divine life as communication, sharing. He prays, "All that is mine is thine, and what is thine is mine" (John 17:10). His sharing of himself and of all the truth arises from the total sharing between the Father and the Son in the Holy Spirit. The Holy Spirit is sharing, communication. . . . Communication is constitutive in the mystery of God. Each of the three Divine Persons possesses all that is good, all that is true, and all that is beautiful, but in the modality of communion and communication. Creation, redemption, and communication arise from this mystery and have as their final purpose to draw us, by this very communication, into communion with God. Creating us in his image and likeness, God makes us sharers of his creative and liberating communication in communion, through communion and in view of communion.[22]

Likewise, Avery Dulles echoes Haring in asserting that the Trinity is "communication in absolute, unrivaled perfection, a totally free and complete sharing among equals" then proceeds to outline how Father, Son, and Spirit engage in this process in particular ways.[23] For Dulles, Christianity and the Church are preeminently about communication, following from God, who "in his inmost essence is a mystery of self-communication."[24] Building on the work of Haring, Franz-Josef Eilers simply summarizes the human and pastoral relevance of God's trinitarian essence: "Why are we as human beings able to communicate? It is because this trinitarian communicating

---

22. Bernard Haring, "Ethics of Communication," in *Free and Faithful in Christ* (New York: Seabury Press, 1979), 155.

23. Avery Robert Dulles, *The Craft of Theology* (New York: Crossroad, 1992), 37ff.

24. Ibid., 38.

God has created us in 'His image and likeness.' Because God is a communicating God, we are able to communicate."[25]

For exploring the theological foundations of communication, the Trinity is thus essential. In pondering the relation of Father, Son, and Spirit, we may, along with Haring, Dulles, and Eilers, imagine God's complete self-giving and self-receiving, mutuality, sharing, freedom, invitation, gift, acceptance, intimacy, co-indwelling, and communion. Though our concepts are limited, imagining God as the communication and communion of the Trinity sheds light on the fullness of what human communication can be if honoring our nature in *imago Dei*. Conversely, human communication that is blind to the possibility of communion results in abuses of dignity, progress, justice, and freedom. As *Communio et Progressio* warns:

> if men's minds and hearts are ill disposed, if good will is not there, this outpouring of technology may produce an opposite effect so that there is less understanding and more discord and, as a result, evils are multiplied.[26]

Salvation history, if read from the perspective of communication, illuminates the importance of adhering to the standard of divine communion in human communication. *Communio et Progressio* alludes, for example, to Genesis 11 and the story of the Tower of Babel: humankind chooses self-reliance over God's providence and becomes unable to communicate because of the confusion of languages. In the story of God's relationship with Israel, communication remains key: we observe the telling and retelling of the story of God's saving love as a way of expressing identity, as well as the periodic rise of prophets who recall and reinterpret for the people God's word in light of their present context. Then, in the fullness of time, God "communicates His very self to man and the Word was made flesh."[27] From the perspective of Christian theology, the height and fullness of God's self-communication to humankind takes place in the incarnation of the Word, in the person of Jesus Christ.

25. Franz-Josef Eilers, *Communicating in Ministry and Mission*, vol. 3 (Manila, Philippines: Logos, 2009), 27.

26. CP 9.

27. Ibid., 10.

Christ, the Perfect Communicator

In paragraph 11, *Communio et Progressio* identifies Christ as the Perfect Communicator. This profound metaphor gathers together the theological threads above: the unitive potential of social communication, the creativity of human communication as rooted in the *imago Dei*, and the nature of God as the communicating communion of Father, Son, and Spirit. As noted above, salvation history as a whole can be told from the perspective of communication with the aim of communion: ultimately uniting people to God and to one another as its final end. Within this salvation history, Christ is the fullness of revelation: the Word and Image of God uttered to humankind in the most intimate and familiar of terms. This revelation is in itself unitive; as *Dei Verbum* explains, "it pleased God, in his goodness and wisdom to reveal himself and make known the mystery of his will (see Eph 1:9), which was that people can draw near to the Father through Christ, the Word made flesh, in the Holy Spirit and thus become sharers of divine nature."[28] Christ's incarnation *is* the engaging invitation to humankind: in taking on human nature, Christ seeks to bring humankind into the divine, eternal communion of Father, Son, and Spirit. As such, the Word of the incarnation brings a message that is wholly, perfectly, and fully aimed at communion.

The theologies of revelation and incarnation are indispensable to the metaphor of Christ the Perfect Communicator. Revelation identifies God's saving Word uttered to humankind throughout salvation history and most fully in Christ. The incarnation is the expression of this saving Word in the most relational of terms with communion as its *telos*. As *Communio et Progressio* notes, in his life, death, and resurrection, Christ "shared with everyone the truth and life of God, and he did this more richly and lavishly than ever before. As the only mediator between the Father and mankind, He made peace between God and man and laid the foundations of unity among men themselves."[29] Thus in his revealed and incarnate nature, Christ the Perfect Communicator already embodies the message: his very being is a communion of human and divine, immanent and transcendent,

---

28. DV 2.
29. CP 10.

historical and eternal. Along these lines, Christ the Perfect Communicator is a symbol of the Good News, the preverbal articulation of the Gospel before it is actually made explicit by his life, ministry, and legacy.

As *Communio et Progressio* identifies Christ as the Perfect Communicator, it also moves into exploring how his life and ministry revealed this about him in explicit terms. As paragraph 11 notes, Christ's perfect communication was total; "not just words but the whole manner of his life." His communication was relevant, bold, and contextual. He was aware of who he was and who his audience was, and he embodied the Good News accordingly. At the root of such authentic communication is the "gift of self in love."[30] Communication as a gift of self in love seeks, at its most basic level, to relate: it is a gesture of bringing oneself authentically to encounter another with an aim of moving toward more profound intimacy. Giving himself in love describes Jesus entirely: from his conception to his death on the cross. It is also an apt summary of his interactions, manner of relating, and ministry. For Franz-Josef Eilers, this "gift of self in love" is paradigmatic for Christian communication and central to ministerial formation.

Reflecting primarily on priestly formation, Eilers envisions communicators "par excellence" who share the Gospel not only through understanding and skill but also through lived basic dispositions and attitudes of God's communication toward us.[31] Here it is helpful to recall that Christ is both Word and Image of God; his Good News is both articulated and embodied as an act of total communication.[32] The repertoire of Christ's perfect communication thus includes the broadest definition of communication: words (conversation, teaching, proclamation), images and symbols (parables, metaphors, symbolic acts), gestures (healing, ministering, reconciling), presence (accompaniment and solidarity with those on the margins), as well as his silence. As Word and Image of God, his total sharing of self is revelatory of God's self-communication. And as revelation, this self-communication always seeks and addresses the human person so that

30. Ibid., 11.
31. Eilers, *Communicating in Ministry and Mission*, 157–58.
32. CP 10.

the person may enter into ever-deeper relationship with God. While Christ accomplishes this perfectly, he also offers a standard for his disciples to follow. As such, Christ's model of total communication continues in the Church, and in fact is constitutive of the Church. As *Evangelii Nuntiandi* reminds us, evangelization, or the total communication of the Good News, is the Church's deepest identity. And it is an activity that takes into consideration the participants, contexts, message, methods, and media of communication.[33]

Communio et Progressio concludes its theological foundations by drawing out the fundamental moral principles that will guide humankind toward communion through the instruments of social communication: freedom of choice (13), dignity of the human person (14), the common good (16), and the importance of truth (17). The theological section ends on an inspiring note, enticing the reader with a hopeful vision of what social communication could be if "completely in tune with the aims of the People of God."[34] The unity of humankind in communion with God is the parting image, a bookend to the beginning of the section, and framing the reflection with this vision of ultimate hope.

Legacy for Ministry in the Digital Age

In articulating a theology of communication, *Communio et Progressio* names communication's role in the human person's search for ultimate meaning, and does so in particularly Christological terms. In the digital age, this theology of communication becomes an invaluable element of dialogue with greater culture: an expression of ultimate meaning that speaks to the enduring spiritual search of humankind. For pastoral leaders and ministers, the theology of communication we have inherited from *Communio et Progressio* provides a way to enter into conversation with digital culture and to bring the Gospel to the spiritual questions expressed therein. Although digital culture may not necessarily associate its ultimate hopes and values with religious tradition, a closer look reveals hopes and values that

33. EN 14.
34. CP 18.

can be appropriately termed spiritual in nature. In the digital culture, humankind continues to seek fulfillment, and the theology of communication as expressed through pastoral and ministerial practice can meet humankind in this search, offering guidance and invitation toward the fullness of life.

Among the ways humankind has expressed its search for meaning in the digital age, two stand out as especially evocative of spiritual themes: trans- and posthumanism, and the negotiation of mediated versus face-to-face presence. Seemingly philosophical threads of digital culture, these in fact find regular expression in our day-to-day communication practices, and express deep spiritual hopes. For pastoral ministry in the digital age, it is valuable to consider where these hopes lie and how the message of the Gospel could speak to them through a practical theology of communication.

Trans- and Posthumanism

Although the terms transhumanism and posthumanism may be commonplace mostly among academic and philosophical thinkers, they reveal an attitude toward technology that is recognizable in a far greater cultural context. Building on classical humanism of the Enlightenment, trans- and posthumanism continue to emphasize the essence of the human person as a thinking being. With the help of technological innovation, transhumanism considers the human person on an evolutionary trajectory from our necessary finitude toward immortality. Transhumanism envisions intellect as eventually liberated from our bodies and, with the help of technology, preserved infinitely in the form of data. Posthumanism is the achieved vision of transhumanism: it is the triumph of technology over human finitude, as our thinking essence remains preserved in hardware and data systems. Some of the classic thinkers of trans- and posthumanism include Ray Kurzweil, Marvin Minsky, and Hans Moravec.

Coupled with this vision is the concept of singularity. As posthumanism elevates technological progress above the embodied potential of the human person, it also assumes that artificial intelligence will one day surpass the intellectual capacity of the human person. The point at which artificial intelligence surpasses human intelligence is called the singularity. Beyond the singularity, the vision of the future is ambiguous, almost unimaginable, but all the while animated by superhuman intelligence.

While trans- and posthumanism and their vision of the singularity may seem like the stuff of philosophical science fiction, they are revelatory of the desire of the human spirit for eternal existence. Shedding the finitude of the flesh and living on forever as essential data expresses, on a fundamental level, a disdain for death and hope for eternal life. Similarly, if technological innovation has ultimate value in the trans- and posthumanist worldview, then the concept of the singularity reveals a desire for communion: unity with that which has ultimate meaning so as to be taken up by it unto eternity. The moment when artificial intelligence surpasses finite human intelligence is the moment when all could become right with the world. At the same time, the mystery of what superhuman intelligence could be is a *mysterium tremendum et fascinans*: a technological utopia that is desirable but at the same time frighteningly unfamiliar in its transcendence. Countless science-fiction thrillers have explored and expressed the possibility of the fascinating yet frightful vision of the singularity.

From the Christian theological perspective, a description such as this is replete with themes of humankind's search for ultimate meaning, a search that is necessarily spiritual and finds its fulfillment outside of itself. Clearest among these is the question of human finitude. The history of faith regales how we have struggled with this question: from the tower of Babel to the example of the Gnostics who sought to transcend the body through special knowledge, we have suffered the body and sought freedom from its limitations through our own means. We may even view the fall of Adam and Eve as the primordial example of humankind seeking to transcend our limitations in order to become like God. Grappling with the finitude of human life and yearning for its transcendence is the essence of the Christ event. In the incarnation, Christ physically assumes our struggle with human finitude; he honors our question by entering into it in with his whole being. His answer to our question is paradoxical: in order to transcend the struggle of human finitude, he enters into it; instead of escaping death he faces it with arms open. It is by his embracing of finitude that he transcends it, and his transcendence paves the way for humankind to follow.

In the trans- and posthumanist vision, technological innovation provides the answer to the question of human finitude. In this sense, these philosophies suggest seeking salvation through our own means. In the digital age, technological innovation can thus imply significance and meaning; being connected ensures safe passage past our finitude and limitations. While the culture as a whole may not articulate its sentiments as "trans- and posthumanism," the normativity of being connected, coupled with the importance now placed on owning the latest and most innovative gadgets, evoke these terms on a lived and practical level. It is on this level that pastoral ministry can most effectively dialogue with and even evangelize these philosophies, offering an invitation from connection toward communion.

For people living and working in a digital culture, constant connectivity is the norm: as our mobile devices allow for communication on the go, there are fewer and fewer contexts in which one is truly "offline." This constant connectivity has many benefits: work communication no longer piles up as it did in the days when one was truly away from the office; old friends and acquaintances are no longer forgotten since their social media profiles keep us up to date; killing time while waiting for a plane or appointment can now become productive time (even though connectivity also allows us the choice to idle with Candy Crush); connectivity makes it easy to locate or meet up with friends, communicate in times of emergency, and stay up to date with the latest news. As digital culture manifests these benefits for an increasing number of people, they gradually become normative. If most people in one's social and professional circle are connected through digital media, it becomes a perceived disadvantage for a person not to be. The discomfort of disconnection when one loses a mobile device or runs out of battery power is an indicator of the significance of connectivity in our lives.

Pastoral theologians and ministers may raise the question of whether our increasing reliance on connectivity reveals a spiritual need. In the most positive light, the drive to be connected is an expression of one's ultimate yearning for communion; this is the trajectory of the theology in *Communio et Progressio*. However, when the technological device of social communication gains such importance that when one is without his or her preferred device, he or she feels disconnected and isolated, the theology of communication encounters the philosophy of trans- and posthumanism. The theology of communication places the experience of human relationality at its center, and social communication is one important way to foster this relationality in *imago Dei*. Trans- and posthumanism, by definition, bypass the human and focus instead on the potential of technology, particularly artificial intelligence. Access to the evolution of this artificial intelligence is of ultimate value, which, as an added benefit, enables people to connect with each other. From a theological perspective, what is at risk here is the marginalization of human connection: what seems to be of ultimate value in the posthuman vision is the surpassing of the human in favor of the sources and instruments of artificial intelligence. The singularity as the transcendence of human intelligence into an artificial realm implies unity with the technology, not necessarily with each other. As such, the singularity as the ascent of artificial intelligence may in fact leave human beings separated from each other, especially if a person is not embedded in the artificial intelligence network. One concrete expression of this today is the digital divide, a concept that points to inequality of access to information technology and digital communication. The term distinguishes between inequality of access based on availability of communication technology and the skills necessary to use it, and factors in age, gender, education, and socioeconomic status as significant contributing elements.[35] Along these lines, according to May 2013 data from the Pew Internet and American Life Project, 15 percent of American adults are not online and thus are digitally divided from 85 percent of the adult population.[36] The resulting marginalization in social participation for this 15 percent is a political, educational, economic issue, as well as a pastoral and ministerial one.

The centrality of technology in communication raises complex pastoral and ministerial issues. As noted above, communication technology carries important benefits, and thus to reject it completely is both an isolating measure and one that is inconsistent with the Church's thought on social communication. At the same time, the theological vision of maintaining the person-in-relationship at

---

35. Neil Selwyn, "Reconsidering Political Popular Understandings of the Digital Divide," *New Media & Society* 6, no. 3 (2004): 344–45.

36. Kathryn Zickuhr, "Who's Not Online and Why," *Pew Internet and American Life Project*, September 25, 2013, http://pewinternet.org/Reports/2013/Non -internet-users.aspx, accessed April 7, 2014.

the center of social communication continues to animate the pastoral and ministerial task. At any point when communication technology isolates instead of connects, divides instead of unites, and raises boundaries instead of building bridges, pastoral theology and ministry have important, prophetic roles to recall the standard of persons-in-relationship. The ethical and moral standards that resonate throughout *Communio et Progressio* are expressions of this prophetic role. On the most practical level, pastoral theology and ministry are thus called to be intentionally aware of who is at the margins of communication because of the digital divide and implement ways to enable access for participation in the life of the community in and outside of the Church. This means that instead of focusing only on the most innovative communication technology, we might instead consider a broad range of technologies to reach more people: mailings, the bulletin, phone calls, announcements from the pulpit, the web site, and social media accounts, all complementing each other in a comprehensive ministerial communications effort.

Mediated Presence

While posthumanism's decentralization of the person can risk isolating those without access to the technology, being connected to technology can also raise boundaries to relationships. In her 2011 book *Alone Together: Why We Expect More from Technology and Less from Each Other*, MIT psychologist Sherry Turkle observes how technology is reshaping our sense of boundaries and manner of interactions with one another.[37] Although she does not use trans- and posthumanist terminology, her observations are akin to the vision of these philosophies. Based on her research in human-artificial intelligence encounters, she concludes with evidence for a surprising human affinity for the company of artificial intelligence: people finding important and valuable companionship when interacting with robots.[38] Likewise, she narrates through numerous case studies how communication technologies have led us to eschew face-to-face or even voice-to-voice encounters

---

37. Sherry Turkle, *Alone Together: Why We Expect More from Technology and Less from Each Other* (New York: Basic Books, 2011).
    38. Ibid., 103–47.

with those around us: often, we would rather text or e-mail than call or seek a conversation in person.[39] The technology that has enabled us to connect, she shows, is now the technology that mounts barriers to our connections; we enjoy the efficiency of communication technologies but have reinserted our own boundaries into the communication dynamics they create.

Negotiating face-to-face versus mediated presence in the digital age is another theologically complex issue. Christian theology holds up "face-to-face" as a standard of ultimate communion with God. While seeing God "face-to-face" in the Old Testament implied a dangerously overwhelming encounter with God's holiness (Gen 32:30; Exod 33:20), God's face also implied blessing (Num 6:25; Ps 27:8-9). In the New Testament, seeing God face-to-face suggests eschatological fullness (Matt 18:10; 1 Cor 13:12). Likewise, in human-to-human interaction, the writers of the New Testament occasionally raised the face-to-face encounter to the highest standard, signaling that written letters were only second best to this (2 John 1:12; 1 Thess 2:17).

Christ as Perfect Communicator also recalls the face-to-face dimension of ultimate communion with God. The theology of incarnation implied within this metaphor underscores the importance of meeting face-to-face; Christ taking on human flesh is the divine move toward this face-to-face encounter with humankind, so that in its fulfillment, humankind may ultimately behold the divine countenance. The tradition of contemplative prayer likewise articulates experiencing intimacy with God in terms of a mutual gaze that lets us see God while letting God see us.[40] Seeing God "face-to-face" is expressing, in metaphorical language, a desire for the fullest of intimacy we know as humans. While Christian hope maintains this standard as our ultimate desire, God's presence remains mediated to us in our human experience. As such, while awaiting in hope the divine gaze, we still experience God's intimate love as mediated through a spectrum of human experiences: creation, history, relationships, community, virtue, goodness, beauty, truth. Catholic sacramental theology hinges on this principle of God's mediated presence through the visible, tangible elements of life.

39. Ibid., 187–209.
40. *Catechism of the Catholic Church*, 2715.

The Christian theological standard of what it means to be present is thus complex. The incarnation of the Word teaches us that the fullness of God's presence is personal, relational, "face-to-face." Yet, in his absence, the risen Lord continues to be present in mediated ways, such as through the communal sacramental celebrations of the Church. For human communication, especially in pastoral and ministerial context, Christ as Perfect Communicator offers a multifaceted model of presences to emulate, ranging from the face-to-face presence of the incarnate Jesus Christ, to the mediated, absent presence of the risen Lord that we experience as Church. This multifaceted model is hierarchical: the fullness of divine presence is face-to-face, while Christ's sacramental mediated presence, though wholly real, still awaits "the fullness of his glory."[41]

What implications does this have for pastoral theology and ministerial praxis in the digital age? Social communication in the digital age has shed new light on the question of mediated presence and has invited our culture into experiencing new mediated presences through our communication practices. In our digital culture, there is a multitude of ways of being present and absent. Two people, sitting side by side and both communicating with others on mobile devices are simultaneously present and absent to each other, and to the people they are communicating with digitally. While communication technologies have greatly expanded how we can be present to other people, how this is reshaping our physical, interpersonal interactions is a lamentable development according to scholars like Sherry Turkle. Our various digital screens have now become boundaries to our face-to-face interactions.

Intentionally raising the screen as a boundary to face-to-face presence may in fact be a coping mechanism. The multitude of ways we can be present to one another in the digital age are replete with possibilities for connection. But they can be overwhelming as well. In a connected context that is always "on" and makes us always reachable, devices allow us to control and manage our interactions intentionally. By contrast, the experience of our sheer, physical presence in the company of another person lacks these "controls"; we can turn our devices off or terminate our mediated presence easily

41. As expressed in the language of Eucharistic Prayer III.

and even abruptly when online, but we cannot be fully absent while sitting next to someone, as our bodies necessarily situate us in their company. Opting for the mediated presence over the physical one may simply be a sign that we are overwhelmed and are trying to manage in a culture that is information saturated.

In the context of our information-saturated culture, pastoral theology and ministry offer the possibility for an ecology of faith that makes room for multiple presences within the overall vision of the community. In her 2013 book *Faith Formation 4.0: Introducing an Ecology of Faith in a Digital Age*, Julie Lytle emphasizes the concept of an ecology of faith as "interdependent components that form people, particularly in faith, through a web of relationships."[42] When it comes to our digital culture, Lytle likewise describes a broad spectrum of communication in ministry:

> An ecology of faith recognizes a wide assortment of elements that invite seekers and form members within a faith community. These typically include a wide range of opportunities to strengthen one's faith through personal and communal prayer, worship, teaching/learning, guidance, healing, service/outreach, enablement and advocacy. While many of these elements will be included in every community's evangelization and formation approaches, pastoral leaders need to tailor elements to fit their unique context.[43]

Within this spectrum of ways, we can likewise imagine the use of a variety of media, ranging from face-to-face presence to the printed word, from electronic newsletters to social media presence. In an ecology of faith, pastoral ministers recognize that it is a combination of these presences and a layering of these media that communicates the message. At the same time, the ecology is not made up of equal parts—the standard of Christ the Perfect Communicator maintains the centrality of the person-in-relationship. Striving for the fullest expression of this is the task of the minister. In different contexts, this full expression may look different—a bulletin sufficiently presents the news and announcements that inform the community, but a pastoral

---

42. Julie Lytle, *Faith Formation 4.0: Introducing an Ecology of Faith in a Digital Age* (New York: Morehouse, 2013), 118.
43. Ibid., 126.

call to a person in hospice demands direct presence. Discerning the appropriate medium for the message of the Good News thus hinges on context: on determining how to best be present to particular contexts and the people one serves. In determining the best medium, the pastoral leader or minister may take into consideration the following:

- What media access and media literacy does the intended recipient/communication partner have?
- What is the purpose of the communication? Is it informative, practical, pastoral, ritual, educational, or some combination thereof?
- Is the communication individual or directed to a group?
- Is the communication one-way or interactive?
- Is this public or private communication?
- What is the pastoral/ministerial need that this communication is addressing or responding to?
- Is there grave concern, serious need, or demand for a decorum of respect and reverence?

In an ecology of media and faith, context shapes communication. In general, the more serious or meaningful the need is and the fewer people it concerns, the more it might be desirable to convey one's direct, face-to-face presence as the medium of communication. However, one can imagine various exceptions to this, such as the necessity of being physically present while presiding at liturgy, even though the recipients of the communication means the whole assembly. Likewise, when ministering to those in grief, face-to-face presence seems most appropriate, but reaching out by mediated communication can also be a way of respecting boundaries during a sensitive time. In addition to this, presence does not necessarily need to imply verbal communication; a ministry of presence can mean accompaniment and solidarity through touch or through simply sharing the space or situation of a person. Awareness of context is thus essential as part of discerning the pastoral approach to communication in the digital age.

In addition to situating pastoral and ministerial presence in an ecology of faith communication, pastoral theology, may also serve a prophetic role in pointing to silence as an essential part of communication. As Pope Benedict XVI offers in his forty-sixth World Communication Day Message:

> Silence is an integral element of communication; in its absence, words rich in content cannot exist. In silence, we are better able to listen to and understand ourselves; ideas come to birth and acquire depth; we understand with greater clarity what it is we want to say and what we expect from others; and we choose how to express ourselves. By remaining silent we allow the other person to speak, to express him or herself; and we avoid being tied simply to our own words and ideas without them being adequately tested. In this way, space is created for mutual listening, and deeper human relationships become possible. It is often in silence, for example, that we observe the most authentic communication taking place between people who are in love: gestures, facial expressions and body language are signs by which they reveal themselves to each other.[44]

In an information-saturated context, silence may be difficult to come by. Yet, as Pope Benedict reminds, it is part and parcel of authentic communication: silence allows for conversation and for the words to resound more richly and meaningfully as they are uttered. Silence in communication is balance: it allows for the flow of information to become a meaningful, mutual exchange between communication partners. Returning to Turkle's observations, we may hide behind gadgets and eschew giving ourselves fully to others in face-to-face encounters because of our constant experience of the flow of information. Boundaries thus might be an expression of our desire for balance, of a way to find our footing in the flow. Pastoral theology and ministry have the opportunity here to offer practical wisdom toward finding that footing another way: by balancing words with silence, speaking with listening, sharing oneself with receiving the other. Christian tradition is rich with spiritual practices that invite meaningful silence as an essential part of balanced and meaningful communication.

---

44. Benedict XVI, "Message for the Forty-Sixth World Day of Communication: Silence and Word: Path to Evangelization," January 24, 2012, http://www .vatican.va/holy_father/benedict_xvi/messages/communications/documents /hf_ben-xvi_mes_20120124_46th-world-communications-day_en.html, accessed April 7, 2014.

Conclusion: A Theology of Communication that Endures

In 1971, *Communio et Progressio* presented a theology of communication that envisioned how humankind might move from connection toward communion with the help of the instruments of social communication. At the heart of this theology is the metaphor of Christ the Perfect Communicator, who teaches us the utter centrality of the human person-in-relationship when it comes to media and communication practices. This theological standard endures, even as the media have changed radically since the promulgation of this document in 1971. As the sections above hope to demonstrate, pastoral theology and ministry continue to plumb the depths of this theology in a digital age, doing so without exhausting its meaning. Trans- and posthumanism, along with the concept of mediated presence, are only two areas where pastoral theology and ministry encounter the deeper questions of digital culture. *Communio et Progressio*'s theology of communication provides a rich foundation for addressing these areas. As the brief dialogue between pastoral theology and digital culture here indicates, these are only a few points where the conversation might start; there is much more to say. The ethos of *Communio et Progressio* makes way for this: the document itself is both a hope for and an expression of continuing conversation between faith and media.

3 ARTICULATING MINISTERIAL FORMATION

Guide to the Training of Future Priests Concerning the Instruments of Social Communication (1986)

The 1986 document *Guide to the Training of Future Priests Concerning the Instruments of Social Communication* offers a slight expansion of the scope of this study thus far. The previous chapters examined documents that focused primarily on social communication and analyzed its implications for Church and society. The *Guide*, a work of the Congregation for Catholic Education with consultation by the Pontifical Commission of Social Communication, is specifically educational in its approach and focuses on priestly formation vis-à-vis the growing importance of new media in our greater culture.[1] Although the document names priestly formation as its intended scope, its content and vision are naturally expandable to lay ministerial formation as well. For the purpose of this study, this *Guide* also comes closest to the dialogue between social communication and ministerial formation that is our special focus. After offering an overview of its structure and main points, this study moves to analyzing the *Guide*'s implications for internet-mediated communication in our digital context.

---

1. The "Commission" changed to the present "Council" in 1989.

Context and Key Points

The *Guide* is a practical response to the initiative to implement ministerial training in social communication, as articulated in both the social communication documents and some priestly formation documents; the document specifically cites *Inter Mirifica* 16, *Communio et Progressio* 111, and the Congregation for Catholic Education's 1970 priestly formation document *Ratio Fundamentalis* 68 to situate this intention. In its practical approach, the *Guide* is thoroughly educational in purpose: it offers a systematic vision of media education for priestly formation (1–28), an exhaustive annotated bibliography of previous ecclesial teaching on social communication (Appendix 1), and a comprehensive list of curricular elements toward establishing a thorough formation program (Appendix 2). For its practicality and comprehensiveness, the *Guide* is thus an invaluable starting point for educators in seminaries and similar formation contexts.

In paragraphs 4–6, the *Guide* offers insight into its own genesis. It is a document that emerges out of the generative tension between magisterial vision and practical realities. After the directives of *Inter Mirifica*, *Communio et Progressio*, and the 1970 priestly educational document *Ratio Fundamentalis*, seminaries and similar institutions of Catholic ministerial formation were left with the task of incorporating mass media education into their curricula. To follow up on this directive, the Congregation for Catholic Education performed a worldwide seminary assessment in 1977 "to ascertain whether and to what extent its directive to introduce a training programme in the field of social communication had been understood and implemented."[2] The Congregation found that in general:

> Definitive and organic programmes were still almost totally lacking, either because of the specific object and scope of any programme was poorly understood, or because there had been a failure to distinguish between the aims and levels which had been visualized in the proposal. A further difficulty was that qualified staff to prepare and carry

2. *Guide to the Training of Future Priests Concerning the Instruments of Social Communication*, 5.

out the training programme in communications were short in supply. Yet another factor was an absence of technical and economic means.[3]

Thus, the magisterial vision for comprehensive formation in social communication met such practical hurdles on the ground. In response, the Congregation collaborated with the then Pontifical Commission for Social Communication to create the *Guide* and pave the way toward overcoming these difficulties.

One notable difficulty, as quoted above, was that media and social communication continue to endure as all-comprehensive and fluid topics, and as such, it is a challenge to easily distinguish "object and scope" or "aims and levels" for training on the practical level. This fluid focus was a difficulty that the council fathers of Vatican II already faced when deliberating *Inter Mirifica*, resulting in the brief final version of that document that primarily sought to invite more conversation. *Communio et Progressio* developed the conversation with a broad scope, and in terms of formation, it emphasized its importance but did not offer specific steps for planning. As the Congregation's assessment indicates, seminaries and similar educational institutions were likely left with the impression that the topic of social communication was important. But at the same time, it also left them with a sense of ambiguity regarding how to proceed given the limits and possibilities in each local context. The *Guide* therefore offers as much systematic clarity as is possible for a document written for a global church. Local dioceses would still need to do the work of contextual adaptation, but the *Guide* left this to them and provided a workable and practical starting point. Two decades later, in our digital context, seminary and lay formation programs still can benefit greatly from this systematic clarity, given that our evolving media landscape demands ever-new formation opportunities.

Levels of Training: Basic

The *Guide* offers a threefold structure for approaching ministerial competency in social communication. Addressing the difficulties laid out in the 1977 seminary assessment, the *Guide* clearly distinguishes

3. Ibid.

between three levels of formation, with aims that range from establishing a basic foundation to forming skilled expertise for ministry in media work. The basic level (14–19) is a foundation that the *Guide* envisions for all "receivers" of media, as it presents an educational ecology of family, school, and catechesis as the formative context for this.[4] Seminary education builds on, or if needed, supplements this basic foundation to bring about a basic media awareness or literacy in learners. This media literacy is coupled with "doctrinal and ascetical training," as the point is not just to gain a clear understanding of the media, but rather to develop the habit of interpreting media vis-à-vis faithful and virtuous living. Thus, this basic media education seeks to develop a lens so that the Christian "receiver" can perceive and interpret a medium and decide whether a particular message is virtuous and life-giving or harmful and detrimental to the human spirit.

Both doctrinal and ascetical dimensions are necessary for this lens. Doctrinal competency helps toward understanding what is good, beautiful, and true in light of the Gospel message, and clarifies the moral and ethical implications around communication that are essential to the architecture of the social communication teachings of the Church. Doctrinal competency also helps on a more specific level, especially as the messages of the media tackle tension points between faith and culture. In addressing a tension point, secular media can vary in the depth of their exposition of the Church's position, and can at times oversimplify, misinterpret, or gloss over the position of faith, while at the same time depicting a credible context for this straw position. Doctrinal training helps "receivers" to be aware of the complexity of these tension points and recognize when depth is lacking in the presentation of the message. If such recognition leads to real dialogue, both the person of faith and greater culture are better for it.

Ascetical training is also integral to a basic ministerial media competency. The *Guide* makes special note of ascetical training as part and parcel of priestly formation, evoking the evangelical counsels and the relative simplicity of life necessary to live out this vocation. Those vowed to the evangelical counsels of poverty, chastity, and obedience face real risks in the modern media landscape, with the

4. Ibid., 15.

overconsumption of media potentially posing a real spiritual hurdle to the fullness of this vocation.

The notion of ascetical training as crucial to ministerial media competency is applicable to the lay vocations as well, especially when considering the correlation between "receiver" and "consumer" in mass media. Robert White illustrates this correlation by rooting the "mass media" and its various instruments in the penny newspapers of the 1830s, which gradually gave rise to the popular media as an institution. Along these lines, White characterizes the popular media as consumption-based and therefore seeking to both capture and entertain the audience with the latest and newest information.[5] Following from this perspective, it is integral to the popular media that the audience keeps watching, reading, listening: the viability of the media depends on it. From the perspective of the audience/consumer, this is not necessarily a negative, especially if what the media offers is useful and desirable for informing, entertaining, and educating. However, White's characterization highlights how the fundamental thrust of the popular media may deemphasize balance and moderation regarding its own consumption; "more" is always better. In light of this, ascetical training in the context of formation makes broad sense, encouraging the Christian to be aware of the media's consumption-based foundations and to insist on a broader ecology of communication that also includes reading, study, silence, meditation, as well as community dialogue and prayer.[6]

The basic level of social communication training is really training for acute cultural awareness. It is the sustained exercise of reading the signs of the times to the extent that they are expressed by media culture—especially as comprehensive social communication instruments gain ever-greater prevalence. Beyond being simple tools, the media have had a profound cultural impact. Basic training in a formation program invites the minister to recognize and characterize media, not just as instruments but as a culture, all with the aim toward effective

5. Robert White, "Mass Media and Culture in Contemporary Catholicism: The Significance of Vatican II," in *Vatican II Assessment and Perspectives Twenty-Five Years After (1962–1987)*, ed. Rene Latourelle (Mahwah, NJ: Paulist Press, 1989), 583–86.

6. *Guide* 19.

ministry within this cultural context. On the most fundamental level, then, the basic level of training aims for competency in engaging in dialogue between faith and culture in a way that enhances ministry, the Christian life, and greater culture as a whole.

Pastoral

The basic competency to engage in faithful dialogue with media culture moves to the next pastoral level of social communication training when awareness yields concrete activity in a ministerial context. According to the *Guide*, pastoral training in social communication aims for the competent use of social communication instruments in pastoral activity; the ability to teach, guide, or train others regarding faithful social communication; and the ability to adapt in ministry to the fluidity of the media-culture landscape.[7] These three main areas of pastoral competency build on basic media-culture awareness and imply a hands-on approach to exploring this aspect of culture. Social communication in a pastoral context has thus moved beyond dialoguing with what media are in our greater culture and gives these a home in the Christian ministerial context. As a result, the Christian context will generate its particular expressions of social communication, even as far as a media subculture after the vision of a particular faith community.[8] Christian social communication, as exercised or guided by the pastoral minister, may differ from social communication as a whole due to its intentional rootedness in Christ the Perfect Communicator and the subsequent moral and ethical implications of communicating fully and as gift of self and an act of love. In this, Christian social communication becomes a dialogue partner again with media culture, offering a witness to the Gospel in the medium, method, and message of Christian social communication.

Under the concrete elements of pastoral training, the *Guide* envisions effective public communication skills, such as speaking and writing to a massive public audience. The *Guide* makes mention of

7. Ibid., 20.
8. White, "Mass Media and Culture." White refers to the difference between Roman Catholic and Evangelical approaches to the media, and media subcultures for ministerial aims. See pp. 589–92.

training for presiding at liturgical ceremonies if and when these are televised or broadcast. This specific example helps to clarify and con- textualize the public role of the pastoral communicator. Before mass media and social communication, the liturgy was the original public communications medium of the Church. It remains so today. As the Church's public and official medium, the liturgy already contextual- izes the presider and ministers in a particular culture, signified by language, dress, decorum, and an overall public presence.

Exploring how formation for liturgical presence can enrich forma- tion for social communication in the public sphere is a rich intersection for further exploration. Although presiding or serving at Mass and giving an interview are two clearly different contexts and purposes, the public presence of the liturgical minister in its essence emerges out of a context where Christian identity is most profound. Carrying some of this identity over to other types of public pastoral presences communicates deeply, even before the minister articulates a particular message. Thinking about how the "medium" of the minister com- municates the "message" of Christ in the liturgy can illuminate the concept of public presence in a new way. It helps to translate this pres- ence over to a broader public context in such a way that it becomes relevant and appropriate for these as well. On a more practical level, it is in the context of liturgical formation that seminarians and ministry students become skilled in public speaking and sustaining a public presence. Pastoral training for social communication can build on these foundations, both practically and theoretically.

While the basic level of social communication formation is clearly intended for all Christians, it is somewhat less evident how com- prehensive the second pastoral level ought to be. Following from *Inter Mirifica* and *Communio et Progressio*, what the *Guide* describes as pastoral training ought to be integral to seminary and ministe- rial formation, helping every student in these institutions develop a foundation in practical, ministerial social communication. Even so, it is possible that in some pastoral contexts, because of geographical, economic, or educational limitations, occasion for ministry through instruments of mass media rarely comes up. In contexts such as these, ministerial formation understandably focuses elsewhere. Yet, with the advent of digital media, social communication has shifted away from sheer instrumentality toward a culture marked by an increasingly participatory experience. Even in rural, low-income and low-education contexts, digital media use is on the rise, especially through smartphones and similar mobile media.[9] As such, pastoral formation for social communication now faces a more ubiquitous cultural experience than the rare occasion of giving an interview to a newspaper or going on television or the radio as part of conveying a ministerial presence.

With the advent of digital culture, pastoral social communication formation also aims to assist in training the minister in the increasingly important task of offering guidance to Church and society about media use and media presence. The *Guide* envisions this role as it articulates the aim "to train [students] to be masters and guides of others (receivers in general, educators, all those who work in the mass media) through instruction, catechesis, preaching, etc., and as consultants, confessors, spiritual directors."[10] As master and guide, the pastoral minister is tasked with helping to establish for others the basic foundations in media literacy outlined above, especially in terms of communication practices toward faithful and virtuous Christian living. As it does with other aspects of pastoral expertise, authentic guidance comes from wisdom gained through lived experience; in order to guide people effectively, the minister relies on lived familiarity with these media, especially as gained through pastoral praxis. Furthermore, the fluid and participatory nature of digital culture shapes this guiding role as one of co-participation with learners, of conveying a sense of ongoing learning and developing wisdom, even on the part of the expert.

In the digital context, this necessity of ongoing experience is a blessing and a challenge. Lived familiarity implies hands-on participation in the new media culture, which remains fluid and evolving. Along with the changing technology, digital media are also popular media that place a high value on entertainment and ever-new content. For example, social media analysts estimate eighteen minutes as the

9. According to the Pew Internet & American Life Project 2012 report on internet adaption. See Kathryn Zickuhr and Aaron Smith, "Digital Differences," Pew Internet & American Life Project, April 13, 2012, http://www.pewinternet .org/Reports/2012/Digital-differences.aspx, 1–2, accessed April 7, 2014.
    10. *Guide* 20b.

average prime of life for a tweet, a figure larger or smaller based on the number of one's followers.[11] Thus, in order to stay relevant on such a digital platform, a considerable commitment of time and presence is required. Recalling the introduction of this study, this sense of considerable commitment is what overwhelms and intimidates many pastoral ministers about the digital media. When it comes to being a credible guide for people from a faith perspective, figuring out a balanced approach to gaining lived familiarity with the digital media remains a challenge. Yet, in this challenge is also a blessing.

Given the fluid nature of digital media, pastoral ministers are not the only people feeling overwhelmed or a step behind. In this context, instead of having all the answers, the guiding role of the pastoral minister might instead be to create a shared space for acknowledging our diverse experiences with digital media and facilitating for the community the pooling of wisdom, resources, and best practices along the way. In this, the pastoral minister still remains an expert guide who can bring the wisdom of theology, spirituality, morality, and ethics into the conversation, while acknowledging that when it comes to the digital media, we are all figuring it out together. Guiding the community toward this is a powerful emphasis on the trajectory of the theology of communication that seeks to move people from connection toward communion.

Expert or Specialist

The third and most specific level of training in social communication is reserved for those who seek to exercise their ministry specifically in media contexts or those who will assume expert or leadership roles at the intersection of media and ministry. In the context of all who enter priestly or ministerial formation, the scope of this is comparatively narrow, and as such this section of the *Guide* is the shortest. Those in formation who already work in media, who show aptitude or inclination to do so, or those who plan to teach or assume leadership in local or national communications offices, are

---

11. Peter Bray, "When Is My Tweet's Prime of Life? (A Brief Statistical Interlude)," The MOZ Blog, November 12, 2012, http://moz.com/blog/when-is-my-tweets-prime-of-life, accessed April 7, 2014.

the students that this section of the *Guide* envisions most specifically.[12] To provide adequate formation for this level of specialization, the *Guide* also envisions training centers for media and ministry, either through ecclesial sponsorship or in collaboration with public institutions with such programs.

One question raised in light of the digital media is the potentially growing overlap between the second and third levels of media formation. Naturally, the pool of people serving as seminary professors with expertise in media, directors of diocesan communication offices, or "media ministers" such as Archbishop Fulton Sheen or Fr. Robert Barron is finite and reserved to those called and gifted to serve in these capacities. When considering platforms of social communication such as radio, television, or journalism, this idea of a limited pool makes sense: after all, gaining a public voice through these mass media is something limited to a select few. As such, the narrow access to these means of social communication also yields a limited need for training ministers to the expert communicator level of formation. However, with digital media, this sense of access has changed. The internet as a social communication platform is defined by its access of the many: the networked participation of many voices is essential to the viability of social networking, achieves desirable figures in web analytics, boosts e-commerce, and, overall, animates our experience online. In the simplest terms, the network exists and continues to grow because people take active part in its flow of information. Access and participation of many are integral to the success and sustainability of the network. Beyond "receivers" of the older mass media models, participants of the digital media are both receivers, producers, and communicators, embedded in a network that increasingly invites them to do all.

In this context, it becomes ever-more challenging to draw a line between pastoral- and specialist-level media formation. In a context where more and more are finding a public voice online, all benefit from gaining expert skills in communication, as this will be demanded of them. Not all may be called as "media ministers," but most pastoral leaders will face the intersection of media and ministry in their work given the growing ubiquity of digital culture. To meet

12. *Guide* 27.

this challenge, formation will continue to explore and even extend the boundary between pastoral- and expert-level media formation.

Digital Literacy and Ministerial Formation

Following suit from the *Guide*'s pedagogical focus, if we continue to draw on the wisdom of educational scholarship for the digital context, one key element that emerges is digital literacy. This complex term is a cojoining of a variety of related literacies (computer, technological, information, media, visual, communication), all getting at a person's ability to communicate effectively toward social participation.[13] Along these lines, Martin and Grudziecki offer the following definition:

> Digital Literacy is the awareness, attitude and ability of individuals to appropriately use digital tools and facilities to identify, access, manage, integrate, evaluate, analyse and synthesize digital resources, construct new knowledge, create media expressions, and communicate with others, in the context of specific life situations, in order to enable constructive social action; and to reflect upon this process.[14]

As "awareness, attitude and ability," this definition of digital literacy reveals a multilevel, gradual growth process. Martin and Grudziecki start with "digital competence," which is the basic skill and ability for digital communication. This moves toward "digital usage," when the competence "comes home," finding application within the users' particular or professional context. Digital usage means the user is able to interpret the potential of the medium and apply it in a way most relevant to them. Finally, the highest level of digital literacy is "digital transformation," the ability to engage with the medium creatively and innovatively. In order to enable and empower a learner's potential for social participation, digital literacy education strives to facilitate a learner from digital competence toward digital transformation. Effective and engaged participants in

---

13. Allan Martin and Jan Grudziecki, "DigEuLit: Concepts and Tools for Digital Literacy Development," *Innovation in Teaching and Learning in Information and Computer Sciences (ITALICS)* 5, no. 4 (2006): 250–53.

14. Ibid., 255.

our digital culture not only are competent in digital media skills but also are able to adapt these skills for their own use and transform these skills toward creative and innovative application. Notably, this threefold schema does not differentiate between basic or specialist users, but seems to envision this trajectory for all learners.

Putting this in dialogue with the *Guide*'s threefold vision of media formation, the initial parallels are evident: both start with basic competence, move toward professional adaptation, and arrive at highly skilled media expertise. However, the *Guide* and the definition of digital literacy also emphasize the highest level slightly differently. As we have seen, the *Guide*, like a pyramid, envisions on its top a small, distinct cadre of media ministers and experts, without the assumption that all might seek to rise to this level from the lower tiers. Born out of the digital cultural milieu with its emphasis on collective, collaborative participation, digital literacy's highest tier holds an invitation for all. Digital creativity and innovation is less tied to a cadre and more connected with a person's comfort with the medium for authentic and novel self-expression. In this dialogue, the *Guide*'s practical vision that, in reality, only some will become media experts in the traditional sense meets the digital culture's evolving sense of what media expertise means in new communal contexts of creativity and innovation.

In a formation program, educating more broadly toward digital creativity as opposed to only toward specialized media expertise may offer a more engaging vision. Educating toward creativity has strong roots in the Church's essential identity and mission. Fostering creativity fosters the minister's ability to participate in the ecclesial process of handing on the content of faith: creativity invites and aids the understanding, appropriation, and reproposition of the Gospel from age to age.[15] Connecting this creative process to the digital media establishes a profound link between this fundamental ecclesial task and the necessity to enact it in the digital age. As such, any educational goal that serves to enhance the learner's creativity in the digital context serves not only their media competency but also their deeper skills for evangelization and pastoral ministry in our greater culture.

---

15. Daniella Zsupan-Jerome, "Creative Communication: Digital Creativity and Theology in Dialogue," *New Theology Review* 26, no. 2 (April 2014): 80–87.

As this is rooted in the fundamental, evangelizing mandate of the Church, it is no small goal. It moves digital communication from a specialized skill set to a necessity for the sake of proclaiming the Gospel. Fostering creativity in ministerial formation to help enable this is indeed a vision for all.

4 TWENTY YEARS LATER

Aetatis Novae: Social Communications on the Twentieth Anniversary of *Communio et Progressio* (1992)

With seven years and multiple drafts of preparation, the pastoral instruction *Communio et Progressio* is, in modern history, the Church's magnum opus on social communication. However, in terms of longevity, its very topic is its Achilles's heel. The rapidly evolving technology of our recent history necessitates continued conversation about the communications media that shape our culture. New media are constantly broadening the horizons of what it means to be connected to and present with one another, to share knowledge and grow in understanding. Between 1971 and the late 1980s, the world of technology saw the emergence of the video game, the personal computer, the mobile phone, videocassettes and CD-ROMs, the Walkman, and virtual reality—all examples of bringing technology to the average consumer so as to enable personalized and individual forms of use for entertainment and communication. With conscious awareness of these new signs of the times, the Church once again returned to the topic of social communication, continuing the conversation with the 1992 "Pastoral Instruction *Aetatis Novae* on Social Communications on the Twentieth Anniversary of *Communio et Progressio*."

History and Context

As its title indicates, *Aetatis Novae* emerged as a commemorative addendum to *Communio et Progressio*, published for that older document's twentieth anniversary. Franz-Josef Eilers notes that by comparison to the elaborate preparations leading up to *Communio et Progressio*, this commemorative document required much less time.[1] Work on the document began in 1986 with a questionnaire circulated to bishops' conferences that sought feedback on this topic, among others. In 1987, at its plenary assembly, the Pontifical Commission for Social Communication raised and explored the question whether to publish a supplement to *Communio et Progressio*, especially in the light of the technological advances in social communication between 1971 and the late 1980s.[2] Between 1988 and 1992, the commission and its expert consultants worked on *Aetatis Novae*, which was published on February 22, 1992. As an ecclesial document, it carries the signature of the commission's president, John Foley. In contrast with *Communio et Progressio*, *Aetatis Novae* does not carry a new papal endorsement, indicating perhaps that as a commemorative addendum, *Aetatis Novae* is not to be read apart from *Communio et Progressio*, and thus implicitly carries on that older document's mission, purpose, and approval.[3] At the same time, Pope John Paul II's thought, especially his emphasis on evangelization, is woven throughout the document.

Overview

By and large, *Aetatis Novae* reiterates previous ecclesial teaching on social communication, quoting from *Inter Mirifica* and *Communio et Progressio* along these lines, as well as bringing in new insights and teachings, primarily from John Paul II. As its overall approach, the document works from a keen awareness of media not as tools

1. Franz-Josef Eilers, *Communicating Church: Social Communication Documents* (Manila, Philippines: Logos, 2011), 152.
2. For a history of the Pontifical Council for Social Communications, including the above details on the genesis of *Aetatis Novae*, see: http://www.pccs.va/index.php/en/about-us-en/history-of-pcsc, accessed April 7, 2014.
3. See *Communio et Progressio*, 187.

for communication, but as a comprehensive, thought-shaping, and culture-making reality of our time. The introduction of the document reflects this: "today, much that men and women know and think about life is conditioned by the media; to a considerable extent, human experience itself is an experience of the media."[4] This last statement is evocative: it notes how much of what we know about our world is gathered and interpreted for us by the media, but it also hints at the fundamental theological principle of mediation that is at the heart of revelation, our experiences of faith, and even the concept of sacramentality. In this, the statement is a constructive bridge that highlights present reality and also gently hints at its value in light of Christian tradition, reminding that the media are broader than the mass media and means of social communication shaping our world today. In a Christian sense, all human experience is mediated.

Following the introduction, the document is structured into five sections. The first section, "The Context of Social Communications" (4–5) elaborates on the broad sociocultural impact and force of the media, elevating these from a tool toward a comprehensive cultural force. The second section, "The Work on the Means of Social Communication" (6–11) reiterates the theological and practical vision of the Church on social communication, including *Communio et Progressio*'s emphasis on the trajectory from communication to community and communion, as well as the importance of dialogue within and with the Church. This section also reflects the influence of John Paul II as it includes a section on the new evangelization, while quoting from his *Redemptoris Missio* (1990). Echoing *Evangelii Nuntiandi* (1974) as well as John Paul II, *Aetatis Novae* includes the media among other traditional means of evangelization: witness of life, catechesis, personal contact, popular piety, and the liturgy.[5] This explicit connection to evangelization and catechesis is new to *Aetatis Novae*; although *Inter Mirifica* affirms the Church's fundamental duty to proclaim the Good News, it does not use the word "evangelization." *Communio et Progressio* mentions this fundamental ecclesial act but does not elaborate specifically on it.[6] Consistent with *Aetatis Novae*'s overall

---

4. *Aetatis Novae*, 2.
5. AN 11.
6. IM 2, CP 163.

approach to the media as a cultural force, it states that the media vis-à-vis evangelization also need a broad vision: rather than tools, they need consideration as a comprehensive cultural reality. Along these lines, the document echoes *Redemptoris Missio*:

> It is not enough to use the media simply to spread the Christian message and the Church's authentic teaching. It is also necessary to *integrate* that message into the 'new culture' created by modern communications . . . with new languages, new techniques and a new psychology. Today's evangelization ought to well up from the Church's active, sympathetic presence within the world of communications.[7]

This integrative approach presents evangelization and communication as essential dimensions of Church and society, rather than just specific tools or aspects of them. Eilers highlights the benefit of such an integrative approach as he notes that it bypasses the instrumentality of social communication and invites us deeper into the idea of communication as a giving of self in love.[8] Such a deep, integrative approach recognizes communication as constitutive of Church and thus has a keen eye on shifts and developments in communication on a sociocultural level. These shifts will provide necessary opportunities and challenges for ecclesiology, as well as pastoral and ministerial practice.

Finding a balance between keeping an eye on culture and seeking an integrative, theological approach to communication can present a challenge. While Eilers favors bypassing the focus on instrumentality, it is on the level of instrumentality that we can detect in a most obvious way how our culture's communication practices are changing. In the digital age, the cultural discussion is often about the latest social media platform, app, gadget, or other such particularity. In terms of ministerial formation, the scholarship this has generated likewise carries on this sense of particularity and often offers practical wisdom on how to use a specific platform as an instrument for ministry. Toward enriching the dialogue between digital culture and ministry, Brandon

7. AN 11, author's emphasis.

8. Franz-Josef Eilers, "The Communication Formation of Church Leaders as a Holistic Concern," in *Mediating Religion: Conversations in Media, Religion and Culture*, ed. Jolyon Mitchell and Sophia Marriage (London: T & T Clark, 2003), 162.

Vogt (2011), Elizabeth Drescher (2012), and Meredith Gould (2013) are among those who have worked on sharing such a particular approach and practical wisdom.[9]

While immensely helpful for the present moment, instrumental particularity also brings with it the challenge of a short shelf life in the digital age. Platforms of relevance change. For example, in 2014, references to Friendster or MySpace are passé, and even Facebook is sensing the competition to remain relevant with the advent of Snap-Chat, Instagram, Vine, visual social networking, and other new forums. While these comparisons are relative, change and fluidity of platforms is evident. In this context, focusing largely on instrumental particularity is a double-edged sword: it creates hands-on facility with a platform that may also quickly lose its relevance as an online gathering place. Exploring social communication in the digital age in more general and comprehensive terms is another option, one that has offered a more stable place for theology to enter the conversation. Conversing with digital culture in such terms allows for the recognition of larger trends and broader patterns, such as the movement toward an increasingly participatory communications culture, the desire toward increasingly visual self-presentation, the fragmentation and integration of online and offline identities and presences, and similar developments. Theology can dialogue with these in a more enduring and more profound fashion than simply exploring how Twitter or Pinterest work and how they might be applied to ministry. At the same time, this general approach of integrating communication, theology, and culture always needs to make room for the particular instruments that exemplify it at the moment. Without this focus, the hands-on experience is lost, risking abstract thought as the only remainder. As such, the challenge for ministerial formation is maintaining a broadly comprehensive vision of digital media *as a culture*, while engaging with the particular expressions of this culture through instruments of digital communication. This in itself offers a generative dialogue, testing and shaping our understanding along the way.

9. Brandon Vogt, *The Church and New Media* (Huntington, IN: Our Sunday Visitor Press, 2011); Elizabeth Drescher and Keith Anderson, *Click 2 Save: The Digital Ministry Bible* (New York: Morehouse, 2012); Meredith Gould, *Social Media Gospel* (Collegeville, MN: Liturgical Press, 2013).

In addition to the problem of the integration of theology, pastoral practice, and social communication, *Aetatis Novae* articulates a number of additional challenges as well (12–15). First among these is the need for ongoing dialogue between the Church's moral and ethical wisdom and the current cultural expressions and experimentations of social communication. In this brief section, the document acknowledges that while its general approach to the media is positive and sympathetic, our cultural experimentation with evolving media sometimes goes awry and results in harm. In the current digital context, cyberbullying and hate speech on comment boards are two examples that come to mind. While appreciating the evolution of media toward ever-new possibilities, the Church's challenge is to remain a conversation partner so as to be able to offer healing wisdom for developments such as these. As the document notes, part of this healing wisdom is the regard for solidarity, human development, passion for the truth, liberty, human dignity and authentic culture, equal access to information, justice, and the common good. *Aetatis Novae* also reiterates that communication is a basic human right common to all. This ethical point also underscores the overall integrative vision of communication in this document, both in Church and in society. To communicate is essential not only to the mission and identity of the Church but also to the human person and community.

The scope of the remainder of the document is pastoral. It considers "Pastoral Priorities and Responses" (16–19) and "The Need for Pastoral Planning" (20–22); it also envisions a draft of the necessary "Elements of a Pastoral Plan for Social Communications" (Appendix, 23–33). Among its pastoral priorities, the document underscores the value of a media ecology for catechesis and evangelization. We find here a kind of pushback against the newer-is-better mentality often found in consumer culture, as the document highlights the value of grassroots, traditional, and folk media as a part of this ecology for handing on the faith.

As compared to *Communio et Progressio*, Eilers notes that *Aetatis Novae* "seems to go a step further in recognizing all means of social communication in society," including what is most traditional.[10] In the twenty years after *Communio et Progressio*, art, music, film, theater,

---

10. Eilers, *Communicating Church: Social Communication Documents*, 152.

and other visual media experienced the development of a variety of creative cultural movements; important among these was postmodernism. Postmodernism reflected deliberate fragmentation and reintegration of form and an intentional deconstruction of "mainstream" culture and values, including a critical commentary on consumerist culture as well as on aspects of technologization. While a thorough overview of the postmodern movement is well beyond the scope of this study, it is telling that *Aetatis Novae*'s renewed emphasis on the return to the traditional, folk, and grassroots emerged out of a cultural context shaped by the postmodern ethos. Arguably, both the return to grassroots and the postmodern deconstruction of the mainstream sought balance over against some of the perceived negatives of the late 1980s; as *Aetatis Novae* lists these: "secularism, consumerism, materialism, dehumanization, and the lack of concern for the plight of the poor and neglected."[11] Elsewhere, the document repeatedly warns against oppressive communication structures (14–15) and the domination of the media elites (15). The return to the grassroots is another expression of this, fueled by both Gospel justice and the postmodern ethos of the era.

Also within the pastoral scope is the ongoing emphasis on education and formation (18), pastoral care for media professionals (19), and keen urgency toward pastoral planning (20–22). The mention of explicit pastoral outreach to media professionals is new: *Inter Mirifica* and *Communio et Progressio* tended to focus on the pastoral, moral, and ethical responsibilities that they carry, while highlighting formation and resources necessary for these. Affirming all this, *Aetatis Novae* goes further, adding that the Church "has a corresponding responsibility to develop and offer programs of pastoral care which are specifically responsive to the peculiar working conditions and moral challenges facing communications professionals."[12] By implication, this pastoral vision folds the work of media professionals into the Gospel; no longer are they just carriers of the message through the various media, but, through pastoral care, the Gospel addresses them as well, personally and professionally. This pastoral care emphasis

11. AN 13.
12. Ibid., 19.

rounds out the vision of formation that has previously focused on the intellectual, moral, pastoral, and technical elements of their work.

The document concludes with an urgent call for pastoral planning. Paragraph 20 echoes the language of John Paul II, naming the mass media as our great contemporary Areopagus. The reference is to Acts 17's account of Paul's visit to the Areopagus, the rocky hill in Athens that was the meeting place of the city's council of elders, connoting both intellectual and juridical significance. Paul preaches there upon request—responding to the intellectual intrigue of the Athenians, whom he affirms as religious (Acts 17:22-23). Building on this shared openness to religious thought, Paul presents to them the Gospel message, eliciting further interest from many and conversion from some. Likening the mass media to the Athenian Areopagus acknowledges the media's sociocultural power as well as its potential openness to the truth of the Gospel. It is a place for exchanging ideas in intellectual pursuit and exploration of the truth. As a metaphor, it brings to mind a sense of dignity and respect for this endeavor, like an academic colloquium or a forum of well-respected experts. The Areopagus of the mass media thus carries a standard of integrity, especially regarding the intellectual pursuit of truth.

When it comes to the digital media, this metaphor becomes less fitting. Pope Benedict XVI used the metaphor "the digital continent" in his 2009 World Communications Day Message. As he encourages young people, "It falls, in particular, to young people, who have an almost spontaneous affinity for the new means of communication, to take on the responsibility for the evangelization of this 'digital continent.' Be sure to announce the Gospel to your contemporaries with enthusiasm."[13] As compared to the Areopagus, "digital continent" brings to mind a different reality. Instead of a council of the respected intellectual elite, continent evokes a sense of embeddedness, an inculturated reality, an entire way of life situated in the digital context. This entire way of life includes the pursuit of truth, playfulness, en-

13. Benedict XVI, "New Technologies, New Relationships: Promoting a Culture of Respect, Dialogue and Friendship." Message for the Forty-Third World Communications Day, January 24, 2009, http://www.vatican.va/holy_father /benedict_xvi/messages/communications/documents/hf_ben-xvi_mes _20090124_43rd-world-communications-day_en.html, accessed April 7, 2014.

tertainment, identity exploration, socializing, commerce, creativity, and more. As opposed to the revered council of intellectual elite, life on the digital continent is complex, imperfect, and messy. As such, the communication of the Gospel therein requires a different standard, a standard of encounter and integration, of participating with people in the digital sphere. To return to the ancient Athenian metaphor, the digital culture invites us to consider not only the Areopagus but also the agora found downhill from it, and bring the Gospel, as Paul did, to both.

Formation for a Participatory Culture

When it comes to pastoral planning—and pastoral formation, as well—the shift in metaphors from the Aeropagus to the digital continent is significant. When *Aetatis Novae* was created, identifying those "in the media" was a more clear-cut task, bringing to mind a professional cadre of people who were trained in journalism, broadcasting, or other forms of communication to a mass audience. Pastoral planning and formation in this context meant successfully engaging with these professionals or with their work for the sake of the Gospel. In this context, the Areopagus is a fitting metaphor, as it refers to this specific cadre and the media profession's ethical task to pursue truth and communicate information truthfully.

When the Aeropagus finds itself on a continent in the digital age, the professional cadre likewise finds itself surrounded by an increasing number of "amateur" public voices who increasingly contribute to the public media discourse, at times with real significance. These amateur public voices are our voices—including pastoral leadership, staff, the Christian faithful, as well as the greater world around us. Communication formation and planning on the pastoral level now involves grappling not only with how to *engage with* the professional media but also how *to be* the amateur media, for the sake of the Gospel, in the digital age. As the boundaries between professional and amateur media continue to shift, pastoral planning and formation will benefit from a broader sense of whose voices are involved and who can help empower the amateur Christian voice toward an authentic proclamation of the Gospel through new media. *Aetatis*

Novae offers impetus for this in its insistence on the common right to communication, including within the Church itself.[14] Building on the assumption that all within the Church have a rightful voice, digital culture now offers us all new public platforms to use it. For pastoral and ministerial formation, this proliferation of public voices is a new opportunity and challenge.

Henry Jenkins's systematic definition of participatory culture is helpful here, especially as we rethink formation for a digital age. In *Confronting the Challenges of Participatory Culture* (2009) Jenkins and coauthors envision a pedagogy that enables learners to participate in digital media culture. Our digital culture is marked by our participation; its instruments have increasingly enabled our presence, creativity, collaboration therein with relative ease. Jenkins's definition of participatory culture is one that is often cited:

> A participatory culture is a culture with relatively low barriers to artistic expression and civic engagement, strong support for creating and sharing creations, and some type of informal mentorship whereby experienced participants pass along knowledge to novices. In a participatory culture, members also believe that their contributions matter and feel some degree of social connection with one another (at the least, they care what other people think about what they have created).[15]

Our engagement with digital culture is a cycle: the culture is generated by our participation, but it also demands it. In light of this, an increasingly essential part of education is to enable and empower learners toward successful and effective participation in a culture that demands this of them. Along these lines, *Confronting the Challenges* names a number of new skills to form for effective participation in digital culture: play, performance, simulation, appropriation, multitasking, distributed cognition, collective intelligence, judgment,

14. AN 10.
15. Henry Jenkins, et al., *Confronting the Challenges of Participatory Culture* (Cambridge, MA: MIT Press, 2009), xi, http://mitpress.mit.edu/sites/default/files/titles/free_download/9780262513623_Confronting_the_Challenges.pdf, accessed April 7, 2014.

transmedia navigation, networking, and negotiation.[16] All of these skills help to ensure that a person can contribute in a meaningful way, in a way that they perceive as valuable and valued by others. According to *Confronting the Challenges*, it is this perceived sense of value that is of great importance in participatory culture; not all participants will contribute as actively or in the same way, but the ethos of the community is that, if and when they do, it is welcome and it matters. Accordingly,

> in such a world, many will only dabble, some will dig deeper, and still others will master the skills that are most valued within the community. The community itself, however, provides strong incentives for creative expression and active participation.[17]

This sense of living, active, creative community is a strong attraction for digital participation, dabblers and masters alike.

Regarding pastoral or ministerial formation, an inescapable reality of our digital age is the overlap that emerges between formation for pastoral communicators and basic catechetical formation for all the faithful. In the participatory culture of our new media, no longer are professional ministers the sole communicators of faith; "amateur" voices of authentic faith emerge alongside, and blog, tweet, post, create, and share in the digital context, enabled by technology and energized by the sense that their contributions are valuable. When it comes to formation for communication, this task is not only for the seminary but also for the parish, school, and family. Parallel to the shift in greater media culture, pastoral leaders and ministers who are the Church's "professional communicators of the faith" are finding themselves joined by a growing chorus of amateur voices who are, often for better but sometimes for worse, doing theology online. Formation for communication cannot dismiss this proliferation of public voices, as it raises significant opportunities and challenges for catechesis and religious education.

When it comes to the role of the professional communicator of faith in this context, one gift of participatory culture is the sense of

16. Ibid., xiv.
17. Ibid., 6.

collaboration that it engenders. Collaboration in the digital context calls the minister or pastoral leader to consider how to engage with professional communicators of faith through digital media, how to develop one's own professional voice, as well as how to work with and enable the amateur voices of faith online—all in a way that serves the authentic proclamation of the Gospel in these new contexts.

These new opportunities for collaboration seem challenging, but, if achieved, could also hold great benefits. Clay Shirky sees enormous potential in the new participatory culture wrought by digital media. According to Shirky, the shift from a previously consumer-based media culture to the consuming, producing, and sharing that now marks the culture of digital media invites us into the vast cognitive surplus of humankind in collaboration, previously accumulated and untapped, as we spent our free time parked in front of the television, passively consuming its message.[18] The participatory culture wrought by digital media now invites us back into an active role, not only to consume but also to produce and share content. As Shirky notes, this kind of collaborative sharing is broad ranging: from the silly to the socially conscious, from the creation of "lolcats" (pictures of cats with funny captions) to the Kenyan Ushahidi blog that helped to track and report ethnic violence in 2008. Through it all, people are collectively creating and sharing, tapping into the cognitive surplus to accomplish something. Echoing the work of Jenkins, Shirky summarizes: "To participate is to act as if your presence matters, as if, when you see something or hear something, your response is part of the event."[19]

From the perspective of pastoral and ministerial formation, this summary statement guides us to the profound repercussion of digital culture for our sense of being Church. In a media culture where participation invites and fuels a sense of "presence that matters," formation vis-à-vis the media reaches well beyond the skill set of how to use new social media platforms. Media formation for the digital age invites the pastoral leader and minister to think about facilitating a "presence that matters" for the people they serve, so that each person may contribute to and take part in the sharing of

18. Clay Shirky, *Cognitive Surplus: Creativity and Generosity in a Connected Age* (New York: Penguin Press, 2010), 1–29.

19. Ibid., 21.

the faith authentically and in service of the Gospel message. This sense of "presence that matters" is already engendered by our media culture and offers both a starting point and a new way of thinking about the communal visions and aims of ecclesial ministry. Fostering a sense of "presence that matters," a sense of belonging where one's contributions are valued and important, where one's participation edifies the collective, is language that can also describe the hope we hold for the people we serve in ecclesial ministry.

The Second Vatican Council's ethos for "full, conscious, and active participation" encapsulates this hope, as does the clarity of later documents about the baptismal mission of each person to evangelize, to be part and parcel of the Church's basic identity and mission.[20] For an evangelizing Church, each baptized person has "a presence that matters." Or, to use St. Paul's words: "Now you are the Body of Christ and each of you is a part of it" (1 Cor 12:27). Digital media offer the Church the opportunity for more of the members of the Body to be aware of and claim their full, conscious, and active presence therein.

Digital culture engenders a sense of "presence that matters" in our interactions with new media, while a different kind of communal "presence that matters" is part and parcel of our hope for a vibrant, Spirit-led Church. Pastoral leaders and ministers formed in digital communication are bridge builders between a sense of belonging in participatory culture and what it may hold for the Church. They are aware of this participatory dynamic and can imagine how to adapt it and deepen its potential for the life of the Church and the mission of evangelization. They can think broadly about the vision of a participatory Church, where each member of the Body has a sense that his or her contribution is valued and important. Those who sense this will indeed participate fully, actively, and consciously in all expressions of being Church. This sense of participation in our greater, digital culture thus bears a gift for our practical ecclesiology, a gift that can enrich our sense of community on- and offline.

In terms of practical formation, then, educating for ministry in the digital age implies fostering the ability of the minister to engage in the participatory culture of the digital continent along the lines

20. See *Sacrosanctum Concilium* 14; see also *Lumen Gentium* on the universal call to holiness, paragraphs 40–41; *Evangelii Nuntiandi* 21; *Catechesi Tradendae* 24.

of the skills enumerated by *Confronting the Challenges* above. In addition, it also implies nurturing a critically constructive awareness of participatory culture vis-à-vis our understanding of the Church's evangelizing identity and mission. Putting these together, one critical learning outcome for pastoral formation is to enable the minister to participate in digital culture so that he or she can foster a communal sense of participation in the Church for all the faithful, both on- and offline. Digital media literacy and a clear sense of connection between ecclesiology and evangelization are essential elements of such a vision for formation. In a cultural context where all are offered a public voice, pastoral leaders and ministers of the digital age have a clear call not just to communicate but to facilitate the faithful communication of the people they serve.

5 ARRIVING AT INTERNET-MEDIATED COMMUNICATION

Ethics in Internet (2002), *The Church and Internet* (2002), *The Rapid Development* (2005), and the *World Communications Day Messages*

Thus far, this study has examined the Church's thought on social communication through the lens of key documents between 1963 and 1992, while seeking to articulate the wisdom these hold for our digital culture especially in terms of pastoral and ministerial formation. Moving into the 2000s, the Church began to address internet-mediated communication more directly, both in select World Communications Day messages and through a number of brief documents dedicated to the subject. This chapter focuses on these internet-themed documents, exploring what wisdom they hold for us a decade or so later—especially in terms of pastoral and ministerial formation.

Since the early 2000s, internet-mediated communication has continued to evolve toward a more interactive experience, a shift often labeled from "Web 1.0 to 2.0" and beyond. Social networking, mobile media, application-based platforms, and a continuing integration of our online and offline experiences through these mark the evolution of the internet in our present day. How we communicate—through this one medium—has continued to change dramatically, and yet the articulation of the Church's thought on this medium helps to refine the vision for formation even in this fluid context. This chapter briefly summarizes and draws some implications for formation from these respective documents.

Ethics in Internet (2002) and *The Church and Internet* (2002)

These two sibling documents, examining separately the two major components of the key social communications documents that came before, were published together by the Pontifical Council for Social Communication. *Inter Mirifica, Communio et Progressio,* and to some extent *Aetatis Novae* all followed a similar pattern: articulating a theological foundation, making cultural observations, then presenting practical implications in ethical and pastoral terms. These two sibling documents approach the communications medium of the internet from two related lenses: ethical and ecclesial-pastoral.[1] Both documents are brief, and both stand on the shoulders of the social communication teachings offered in *Inter Mirifica* and beyond. At the same time, each of them offers thoughtful nuances for thinking about internet-mediated communication and the culture it engenders.

Ethics in Internet leads the way, evidenced by how *The Church and Internet* builds on the reflections therein, and cites *Ethics in Internet* a number of times. It begins with and affirms the observation of *Aetatis Novae* that the means of social communication are not mere tools, but rather have fundamentally reshaped our thought, life, and culture. *Ethics in Internet* offers an evocative image: "the earth as an interconnected globe humming with electronic transmissions—a chattering planet nestled in the provident silence of space."[2] This image underscores how much our networks of social communication have imbued our lives, but it also invites our awareness beyond this immediate reality. The provident silence of space reminds us that there is a greater, infinite beyond that always humbles our here and now. The fact that space is silent also hints at balance, that in the midst of our chatter, we cannot let go of the importance of the silent stillness

---

1. *The Church and Internet*, 2–3.
2. *Ethics in Internet*, 1.

that allows our words to resound. The provident silence of space that holds our chattering planet is also evocative of God, whose ever-greater grace surrounds, holds within itself, and animates our human activity. This theme of balance for silence will continue to emerge as digital media evolve; both the 2012 and 2014 World Communications Day Messages address it as integral to communication. Along these lines, *Ethics in Internet* presents its key question as whether or not our interconnectedness is "contributing to authentic human development and helping individuals and peoples to be true to their transcendent destiny."[3] Parallel to this is the fundamental ethical principle of focusing on persons in community: "the human person and the human community are the end and measure of the use of the media of social communication; communication should be persons to persons for the integral development of persons."[4] This standard of the person-in-community remains the ethical and pastoral yardstick by which to measure whether our evolving communication practices authentically convey the Good News. As key ethical aspects of this standard, the document notes solidarity and the common good (4), especially as the realities of globalization (5), transnational corporations (6), privacy, copyright, and fluidity of truth (7) raise new challenges.

Ethics in Internet characterizes the internet as an essentially decentralized and decentralizing communication structure, and one that has potential for both good and evil (8–10). In insisting on the internet's potential for both, the document refuses to either personify it or present it as ever apart from the people who animate its communication networks. The internet's potential for good comes from the goodness of people who seek to communicate toward human dignity, the common good, solidarity, development, and authentic relationality between people. Likewise, the harmful effects of internet-mediated communication come from people intending to communicate to do harm, obscure truth, cause division and isolation, steal identities or the intellectual property of others, or to damage human dignity by pornography, cyberbullying, or by using flaming and hateful language. In pinning the morality of the internet on the people who use it, *Ethics in Internet* remains consistent with

3. Ibid.
4. Ibid., 3.

its persons-in-community standard. It is in the hands of persons to determine whether the internet will become a means of social communication that harms or heals.

As particular areas of concern, the document focuses on the digital divide (11), authentic cultural dialogue (12), and freedom of expression (13). In a sense, all three of these are about ensuring fair access to the medium for all, so that the internet can truly become a shared communications platform. Those who cannot enter the conversation because of lack of resources, education, cultural hospitality, or imposed hindrances on free self-expression present a moral and ethical concern; if the positive potential of internet-mediated communication is truly in the hands of persons-in-communication, then to limit the participation of people limits the potential of all that could be accomplished for the good through it. At the same time, the participation of people brings along with it harmful, offensive, or even criminal behavior, and *Ethics in Internet* lays out the boundaries of necessary regulation of online content vis-à-vis freedom of expression (17). In our present day, these boundaries call for ongoing reexamination.

With the advent of social networking and increased user participation, it becomes difficult to impose a standard of ethics on what people contribute. Online contributions of content come from a range of voices: media professionals with a code of ethical conduct to basically anyone with a computer and an internet connection. As we saw in the previous chapter, contributions freely range from the socially conscious Ushahidi to the lolcat, from expert commentary to memes, from words of affirmation to vile comments. It is no longer plausible to imagine an ethical code of conduct that could rein all these in. The decision falls on individual web sites or platforms to monitor or limit offensive and harmful contributions, and often this measure can only be enacted after the fact.

One example of this tension appears on the papal Twitter account, @Pontifex. The account launched in December 2012 with an invitation from the Vatican to engage with Pope Benedict XVI through sending him questions with the hashtag #AskPontifex. The invitation lit up the Twittersphere, and @Pontifex gained a million followers from the time of the launch to the date set for Pope Benedict to reply, nine days later. #AskPontifex gathered tweets ranging from genuine to irreverent, affirming to angry, pious to rude; all were welcome. In

2014, the @Pontifex account has over 13 million followers, and the variety of voices replying to Pope Francis remains the same: some affirm and appreciate, some mock and strive to offend. The enduring and radical hospitality to all voices is by choice: as the Vatican social media team behind the papal Twitter account weighed the alternatives, they discerned that the act of monitoring and blocking of comments would not communicate the fundamental openness of the Church to all. Instead, they chose to welcome this full spectrum of human expression. Yet encountering this radical hospitality can present an uncomfortable experience, especially for those looking to encounter the pope via @Pontifex with the best intentions and who instead have to also encounter mockery or profanity. This tension is a signal of human expression struggling to find an ethical standard in the digital age in a context where the proliferation of public voices has made imposing any standard on them, even for the good, a challenge.

As if expressing foresight of this, *Ethics in Internet* closes with emphasis on the Church's role as dialogue partner with the culture of communication engendered by our new technologies (19). Rather than dictating decisions and choices, what the Church offers is wisdom to help uphold human and Christian values. The choice remains with each person to engage in communication practices that build up or tear down.

Like *Ethics in Internet*, *The Church and Internet* is also brief and builds on the social communication teachings before it. Along the lines of digital Areopagus and digital continent, *The Church and Internet* introduces a metaphor for human communication in our time: the road. This metaphor is more subtle. It could possibly be understood as a lens through which to view the story of salvation history. *The Church and Internet* names the story of Babel and the confusion of languages (Gen 11:1-9) and Pentecost and the restoration of communication (Acts 2) as two landmarks along this road, and considers our modern means of social communication as "cultural factors that play a role in this story."[5] On this road, communication is a symbol that conveys humankind moving from disorder, confusion, and discord when not in right relationship with God (Babel), to Christ's

5. CI 2.

redemptive work, which leads to understanding and coming together through the communication of the Good News across linguistic and cultural boundaries (Pentecost).

If the means of social communication are cultural factors along the way, there is a long line of them, ranging from oral communication, letter writing, and the printed and illuminated word to mass media, electronic media, and now digital media. To consider the digital media in the long line of all of these alleviates some pressure about how to use them. It reassures us in the fact that the Church has consistently relied on various media to communicate the message of the Good News. The metaphor of the road brings this to the thinking about communication: a history of where the Church has come from, and a direction headed toward the kingdom of God (2). The metaphor of the road continues to be evocative for thinking about digital communication; Pope Francis revisits it in his 2014 World Communications Day Message, approaching it in light of the story of the Good Samaritan.[6]

The Church and Internet is largely concerned with the Church's effective communication of the Good News to the world in supporting and collaborating with modern media and the Church's own internal communication as well. Along these lines, the document situates this concern within the essential role of communication for the Church, echoing some of the theological foundations of *Communio et Progressio*: Trinity, incarnation, revelation, evangelization. From this the document transitions naturally to the internet, citing its expansive reach beyond boundaries as an unimaginable benefit for those who have gone before us to proclaim the Gospel (4). Approaching it as the new rooftop from which to shout the Good News, the document notes the internet's potential for conveying "religious information and teaching" and "direct and immediate access to important religious and spiritual resources—great libraries and museums and places of worship, the teaching documents of the Magisterium, the writings of the Fathers and Doctors of the Church and the religious wisdom of the

6. See http://www.vatican.va/holy_father/francesco/messages/communications/documents/papa-francesco_20140124_messaggio-comunicazioni-sociali_en.html, accessed April 7, 2014.

ages."[7] Considering the Vatican's web presence, such as the main web site www.vatican.va or the more recent www.news.va, the Church's awareness of this potential is clear and practically demonstrated there, as these web sites were built as invaluable portals to access a wealth of such information, news, and resources. Official web sites of national, regional, and local Catholic structures, such as www.usccb.org also fall in line with this resource-portal approach.

Moving from a Web 1.0 toward a Web 2.0 understanding of the internet, *The Church and Internet* also recognizes the medium's ability to connect people. Valuing the internet for "its remarkable capacity to overcome distance and isolation," it is a medium that brings people "into contact with like-minded persons of good will who join in virtual communities of faith to encourage and support one another."[8] In addition to accessing information and resources, the focus here is for people to gain access to each other with the help of internet-mediated communication. In light of this benefit, the aim is no longer about accessing information, but rather experiencing connection toward community. This resonates deeply with the theological trajectory of *Communio et Progressio* and thus is rich in significance for pastoral planning and ministerial approaches. Informing people is an invaluable benefit to digital communication, but thinking also about connecting people in a way that they gain a sense of community online roots pastoral and ministerial efforts firmly within this theology of communication.

One significant question that arises here is how to understand the sense of community that may develop online in relation to the community that gathers in person, face-to-face. Reflecting on whether virtual communities are real communities, Meredith Gould offers the following: "When social media was first developed and everyone got a glimmer about how it might be used, distinctions between real and virtual worlds were helpful. Not anymore. . . . Online communities of faith are real to members who have come to rely on them for inspiration and support."[9] Maintaining the ethical standard of

7. CI 4–5.

8. Ibid., 5.

9. Meredith Gould, *Social Media Gospel* (Collegeville, MN: Liturgical Press, 2013), 27.

persons-in-community articulated in *Ethics in Internet*, and given the potential of internet-mediated communication to connect us not only to information but also to one another, it follows then that the sense of community people can experience online is authentic and real. If it is the human spirit animating the connections we experience there, then these connections can and do convey our presence and invite us into a relational, communal experience online. The digital encounter does bring us into the presence of another person in a mediated fashion, and the spectrum of this mediated presence ranges from the immediate and media-rich experience of a Skype or web conference encounter to the sense of asynchronous presence that an e-mail carries. Insofar as this mediated presence can convey authentic encounter, it can also be a conduit of the grace we might experience through gathering together as community. Pope Francis acknowledged this possibility in the summer of 2013 as he extended the opportunity for gaining an indulgence to all who were present at World Youth Day in Rio de Janeiro, all who watched it or listened to it through broadcast media, and all who followed it through "new means of social communication," such as social media.[10]

At the same time, it is undeniably different to experience the physical presence of another person, as opposed to interacting through a screen. *The Church and Internet* qualifies this difference in terms of experiencing community in our most sacred and profound context: sacramental worship. As the document asserts:

> Virtual reality is no substitute for the Real Presence of Christ in the Eucharist, the sacramental reality of other sacraments and shared worship in flesh-and-blood human community. There are no sacraments on the Internet; and even the religious experiences possible there by the grace of God are insufficient apart from real-world interaction with other persons of faith. . . . Pastoral planning should consider how to lead people from cyberspace to true community and how, through teaching and catechesis, the Internet might subsequently be used to sustain and enrich them in their Christian commitment.[11]

10. See http://www.news.va/en/news/pope-francis-grants-indulgences-for -world-youth-da, accessed April 7, 2014.
    11. CI 9.

In pointing to the sacraments, *The Church and Internet* reminds us of our physicality, our embodied reality, the fact that we are flesh-and-blood, and that our most sacred symbols are made from the stuff of the earth. Interacting through the screen can diminish our sense of this, as our spirit becomes contained in the words and pixelated images rather than in our physical bodies. This is a different kind of embodiment, one that continues to invite our critical reflection as new communication technologies emerge. The incarnational and sacramental emphasis of Catholic theology is indispensable for this ongoing reflection, as these emphases both remind us that there is invaluable mystery to our physicality, such that God chose to enter this physicality in order to invite us into an everlasting human-divine relationship that ultimately transcends it.[12] Therefore, we cannot dismiss the body and what it means to be fully present to someone in light of the body as a portal or icon to the divine.

Insofar as online communities are real, pastoral planners can approach them as integral to fostering a larger, embodied sense of communion. Following from *The Church and Internet*, authentic experiences of community online can lead to deeper commitment to community as it gathers in person. Leading people from cyberspace to true community, as the document suggests, does not necessarily imply a linear path, but rather a cyclical one. Meredith Gould presents this in terms of a "trajectory of engagement" that envisions social media, e-mail, the telephone, and face-to-face meetings as all essential moments along the way to build a connection into a relationship.[13] As she also notes, a face-to-face meeting might come first, and lead people connect through social media as a way to maintain and perhaps deepen their initial encounter. Other times, people might connect to one another online first and grow in relationship in and through these other ways of engagement as well. Cycling through these methods of engagement allows for a number of ways to invite

12. The Catholic eschatological vision never completely leaves the body behind. The risen Christ "kept" his body, though aspects of it were transformed. Likewise, Catholic theology maintains as an ultimate hope the resurrection of the body at the end of time. Transcendence of the body therefore is not a complete abandonment of physicality, but rather a transformation of it so that it is free from the marks of our finitude.

13. Gould, *Social Media Gospel*, 29.

connections; for the pastoral minister, these all offer opportunities
to invite people into true community, opportunities that provide
inspiration and support and honor our embodied reality.

The Church and Internet raises another important aspect of internet-
mediated communication in addressing the authenticity of Catholic
content online. It acknowledges as a problem the proliferation of
web sites identifying themselves as Catholic insofar as they may not
actually be so. The document elaborates:

> As we have said, church-related groups should be creatively present
> on the Internet; and well-motivated, well-informed individuals and
> unofficial groups acting on their own initiative are entitled to be there
> as well. But it is confusing, to say the least, not to distinguish eccen-
> tric doctrinal interpretation, idiosyncratic devotional practices, and
> ideological advocacy bearing a "Catholic" label from the authentic
> positions of the Church.[14]

Along these lines, the document suggests the benefit of some
system of voluntary certification for online materials, carried out on
the local and national level, intended "not to impose censorship but
to offer Internet users a reliable guide to what expresses the authentic
position of the Church."[15] Thinking with this further, this voluntary
certification would be a sign or symbol that indicates ecclesial approval of the content therein, somewhat like a digital imprimatur.
Given the proliferation of Catholic voices, including those with official affiliations and those without, it is difficult to imagine how this
would be logistically carried out, when considering the growing number of platforms online, including social networking, blogs, YouTube
channels, and more. For a blog or YouTube channel of someone's
"unofficial" Catholic voice, each posting and each new video would
require authentication, as social media allows us to engage with these
piecemeal and apart from the original context in which they were
shared. All in all, it is difficult to imagine a system by which these
could all be manageably authenticated as Catholic.

In addition to this immense logistical challenge, it seems that
gaining an official digital imprimatur would be highly desirable and

14. CI 8.
15. Ibid., 11.

therefore forgeable if perceived as an official Catholic stamp of approval. As a visual element, it could easily be copied and replicated by anyone wishing to project this image and thus could lead to dishonest use or even exploitation. The playfulness of the internet easily lends itself to this fluidity of truth, helping to produce mock-Catholic sites and adding to the confusion mentioned by the document. The challenge of confusion around what online is authentically Catholic reflects a shift in understanding religious authority, as traditional authority structures find themselves in the context of an increasingly participatory digital culture. Reflecting on the shifting concept of religious authority online, Heidi Campbell observes that while traditional religious authorities may struggle to exert oversight on the proliferation of religious voices online, new forms of religious authority emerge in those who exercise their voice on their blogs or other unofficial platforms.[16] Some clear examples of these new religious authorities include Rocco Palmo of www.whispersintheloggia.blogspot.com or Lisa Hendey of www.CatholicMom.com, both of whom have fostered an important Catholic online presence parallel to the official authority structure of the Church. In the process of sharing their voices online, these unofficial perspectives have become a new kind of official authority in their own right. Considering the value of their contributions, the challenge of naming the boundaries around what is authentically and officially Catholic online becomes more complex.

From a pastoral perspective, it seems more practical for traditional religious authorities to maintain a clear and accessible online presence and make available authentic and trustworthy resources therein, rather than to attempt to exert oversight on the vast and growing number of public voices online. Along these lines, Pauline Hope Cheong points to a more constructive relationship in seeking continuity between traditional and new voices online: "The logic of 'continuity' involves arguments which propose or reason that the relationship between religious authority and new media is characterized instead

16. Heidi A. Campbell, "Understanding the Relationship between Religion Online and Offline in a Networked Society," *Journal of the American Academy of Religion* 80, no. 1 (2012): 74–76.

by connectedness, succession, and negotiation."[17] Amid all the voices claiming Catholic identity online, the official Catholic voice ought to be clearly recognizable and accessible, such as www.vatican.va, www.usccb.org, or the local diocesan and parish web site, app, or social media presence. Part of the task of digital media literacy training for faith formation is to help people gain access to these, so that in coming across other "Catholic" content online, these official sources can provide a frame of reference. Continuity emerges as people engage with both, interpreting unofficial Catholic content in light of official teaching, while also gaining insight into how official teaching is lived and interpreted in a number of unofficial but authentic ways. In a sense, such digital media literacy training enables people to enter into dialogue between what the Church teaches and how these teachings are lived and interpreted. This is a skilled activity not only in terms of digital communication but also in terms of ministry and approaching the task of evangelization shared by all.

Reflecting on the issues of formation and training, *The Church and Internet* follows the example of previous social communication documents and affirms their importance for all (7, 11). Echoing *Communio et Progressio*, the document emphasizes the formation of young people, but highlights in a new way that the digital media call them not only to be discerning recipients but also active communicators, "learning how to function well in the world of cyberspace, make discerning judgments according to sound moral criteria about what they find there, and use the new technology for their integral development and the benefit of others."[18] This nuance acknowledges a more active role in communication, a role we see heightened today within and through social media. Education and formation for all ages helps people recognize, gain access to, and use their online voice as authentic communicators in the image of Christ the Perfect Communicator.

The Church and Internet is quite direct in reiterating the utmost importance of media training for people serving in pastoral or ministerial

---

17. Pauline Hope Cheong, "Authority," in *Digital Religion: Understanding Religious Practices in New Media Worlds*, ed. Heidi Campbell (New York: Routledge, 2013), 78.

18. See *Communio et Progressio* 67–70 as foundation for *The Church and Internet* 7.

roles. Fear of technology is "not acceptable" (10), and people in these roles "need to," "should," "are obliged to," "ought to," and "must" learn and incorporate media into their approach to ministry (11). In observing such direct language, the message is clear: while the Church is dialogical with greater culture vis-à-vis social communication, internally, there is a heavy and nonnegotiable emphasis that this is necessary.

Technological and sociocultural awareness joins intellectual, human, pastoral, and spiritual formation, so that facility with new media can benefit ministry and enrich one's effort in serving toward the reign of God. Aware that social communication in and by the Church is becoming a shared effort in the digital age, *The Church and Internet* also addresses in distinct sections parents, children, young people, and all people of good will. In this the document echoes *Communio et Progressio* but makes their role and responsibility more explicit, both in formatting and in detail.[19] Recognizing the familiarity and facility that young people have with new media, the document is wise in addressing and encouraging these digital natives to use the internet well—not just as a directive from their parents, teachers, and pastors, but as something they ultimately owe to themselves. In this, the document recognizes and empowers them as important agents of communication. This recognition and empowerment of digital natives continues as an intentional aspect of the Church's teaching on social communication into the 2000s. The web site www.pope2you.net and its related social media platforms—including Facebook, Twitter, YouTube, and Pinterest—exemplify this effort, seeking to engage young people directly and inviting their participation as digital architects into building the Church's online presence. The Pope2You project came online in 2009, parallel with that year's World Communications Day Message from Pope Benedict that especially addressed young people as the "digital generation" and urged them "to take on the responsibility for the evangelization of this 'digital continent.'"[20]

19. Ibid.

20. Benedict XVI, "New Technologies, New Relationships: Promoting a Culture of Respect, Dialogue and Friendship," Message for the Forty-Third World Communications Day, January 24, 2009. http://www.vatican.va/holy_father/benedict_xvi/messages/communications/documents/hf_ben-xvi_mes_20090124_43rd-world-communications-day_en.html, accessed April 7, 2014.

Empowering young people as digital communicators also raises the question of their voice and participation in the Church's official online presence. Through its multiple social media platforms, the Pope2You project is also exploring two-way communication with the Church's official online presence: in 2013, the Pinterest page of Pope2You sought and welcomed user-generated photos intended for Pope Francis, especially from those who could not be physically present in Rio for World Youth Day. Parallel to the Twitter hashtag #AskPontifex, the "My Pictures for Pope Francis" board on Pinterest is an intriguing exploration of how the Church is creating a participatory online community on a global scale.

As *The Church and Internet* concludes, it reiterates the image of Christ as Perfect Communicator, "the norm and model for the Church's approach to communication" (12). From previous social communication documents, this image carries with it the fundamental ecclesial imperative to communicate, the centrality of the person to the act of communication, and the gift of self that is conveyed in an authentic encounter along these lines. Here, *The Church and Internet* sheds light another aspect of communication, as it adds a word of encouragement toward being countercultural. Christ, speaking with his own authority (Matt 7, Luke 9, Mark 1) pursued the path of truth and righteousness at all costs, including breaking cultural norms and testing cultural assumptions when necessary. The image of Christ the Perfect Communicator reveals this aspect of him as well, adhering to the standard of divine self-communication if and when cultural practices may be headed in a different direction. This word of encouragement highlights freedom in Christ—freedom to assess, discern, and act virtuously in a context where it is easy to be carried off by the flow of digital culture.

The Rapid Development (2005)

In his 2005 apostolic letter, *The Rapid Development*, Pope John Paul II commemorates the fortieth anniversary of *Inter Mirifica* by reflecting on social communication in the rapidly changing landscape of the digital age. The letter is divided in five sections, moving from acknowledgement of our digital culture to the vision of hope forward with the help of the Holy Spirit. Along these lines, the first section, "Fruitful Progress in the Wake of the Decree *Inter Mirifica*" (2-3), summarizes and affirms the Church's imperative to consider social communication not just as a tool but as a new culture into which the Church is called to integrate the message of the Good News. Ministries of the Word such as evangelization, catechesis, and other forms of religious education and formation are special areas of the Church's mission where this work of integration is nurtured and carried out. In considering the mass media as cultural force, broader aims of communication also become relevant: solidarity, justice, responsible freedom, and truth—all for the sake of human dignity and development. In assessing the Church's work amid our digital culture and in noting the role of evangelization and catechesis, John Paul II echoes the observations of *Aetatis Novae*.

To elaborate on the Church's continued task, the second section of the letter re-roots it in the theological foundations of ecclesial communication. "Gospel Reflection and Missionary Commitment" (4–6) is a section that is richly dense in theology, evoking the standard pillars of revelation, incarnation, Christ as model of communication, and the Church's task that follows from this. The classic trajectory of communication to communion is also present here, and one on which the letter puts special emphasis, as it notes: "there is however a culminating moment in which communication becomes full communion: the Eucharistic encounter." In situating communication between the revealed and incarnate Word and the liturgical and sacramental presence of Christ, John Paul II invites ongoing theological reflection. In the eucharistic encounter, Word and sacrament communicate Christ's presence, inviting us into a communal encounter to physically receive as sacrament that which has been proclaimed as Word. Both Word and sacrament, as well as assembly and presider, communicate Christ's presence, and in encountering him the ecclesial body manifests his presence for the life of the world.[21]

The act of communion in the eucharistic context signifies the intimate and total encounter between the believer and Christ in the Eucharist, as well as the communal act of unity of assembly as local

---

21. *Sacrosanctum Concilium* 7.

manifestation of the greater ecclesial body over time and space. The eucharistic encounter is thus complex: its physical, local particularity is a necessary portal into the divine mystery that exceeds our here and now. As John Paul II orients us toward this as the culmination of communication, the physical, local, communal elements stand out as especially important when it comes to envisioning communication in a digital age. These physical, local, and communal elements are not an end in themselves but remain necessary pathways into the divine mystery. For communicating faith in a digital culture, this remains an important question and challenge.

From rich theological foundations, the letter moves on to its third section, "A Change of Mentality and Pastoral Renewal" (7–9). Here, the letter by and large echoes previous social communication teaching about pastoral responsibility to consider mass and digital media among the ways the Gospel is proclaimed and integrated into Church and culture. Section four, on "The Mass Media, the Crossroads of the Great Social Questions," follows from this with a broader, dialogical approach to greater culture (10–12). In order to promote the positive development of the media toward the common good, John Paul II envisions a threefold approach: formation, participation, and dialogue. As he briefly elaborates on these three, an emphasis on engagement permeates his vision. Formation here is not specified only as ministerial; rather, the section of paragraph 11 that addresses this seems more comprehensive in its intention, qualifying it as a "vast work." Along these lines, John Paul II names young people as "in even greater need of education in the responsible and critical use of the media," but the breadth of his vision is applicable to Church and society. There are no specific details given about formation, but a number of key words frame the concept: intelligent and appropriate use, human relations, and serving people stand out as essential phrases that underscore a communication as a path to communion.

Participation and dialogue are two related expressions of media engagement. Participation emphasizes the importance of access, not only to information but also to the administration and management of information. John Paul II stresses co-responsibility in this regard, a message that gains increasing relevance with the advent of social media and user-generated content, creativity, and collaboration. At the same time, his vision remains prophetic for digital communication that in our day is largely in the hands of the information technology giants like Google, Microsoft, Apple, and other such major corporations. Parallel to these, we see the development of open-source code, content, and goods, and user-specified copyright options for ease of sharing and collaborating, both strongly motivated by the ethos of true participation in their creation, sharing, and development.[22] As John Paul II stresses co-responsibility with regard to access, administration, and management, it is important to recognize both the corporate and grassroots movements for engaging in digital culture.

Dialogue is an expression of engagement, and John Paul II's vision for dialogue is as a "vehicle for reciprocal knowledge, of solidarity and of peace." In this sense, dialogue is understood to foster a sense of unity among people by forging mutual understanding and facilitating a peaceable society. Concerning the Church more specifically, John Paul II emphasized openness to questions and a constructive dialogue, both within the Church and between the Church and greater society (12). Openness and dialogue inevitably lead to questions of boundaries, as the document reflects on adequate confidentiality in communication, all the while maintaining "timely and sufficient communication about Church events."[23] The simultaneously public/private forum of the internet heightens this challenge, as digital communication can feel private when in fact it unfolds before a massive crowd of possible recipients. For the pastoral leader who uses them, social media platforms and other forms of digital communication join the ranks of other public platforms in that it is generally prudent to envision a larger audience than intended. The reproducibility of digital content may carry one's message well beyond the original context, or one's face-to-face presence may become recorded, reported on, and shared online, with or without the expressed knowledge of the minister. In terms of ministerial formation, raising awareness of the public nature of digital media presence is part and parcel of gaining literacy in the medium.

Awareness of the digital media as a public platform raises some practical questions, such as the challenge of how "official" a person or institution's social media presence ought to be. Social media is

22. See, for example, https://creativecommons.org/, accessed April 7, 2014.
23. *The Rapid Development* 12.

inherently relational and thus especially welcoming of the unofficial voice, but it also offers an intrinsic communication system that
is more timely and effective than other more official means. Pope
Francis's Day of Prayer and Fasting for Syria offers a rich example
of this official potential. In September 2013, Pope Francis extended
a worldwide invitation to a Day of Prayer and Fasting for Syria; the
invitation went out on September 1, a Sunday, and the global day
was set on September 7, the following Saturday. Without a whole
Sunday between the invitation and the set date, local parishes could
not rely on the bulletin or pulpit announcement to raise awareness,
and digital media platforms took on the official role of communicating the message.

In response to Pope Francis's call, the United States Conference of
Catholic Bishops' method of communication was exemplary. Within
two days they created a web site for all information concerning the
Day of Prayer and Fasting but were still left with the challenge of getting the word out. For this they also created a shareable photo of Pope
Francis with a link to the web site and the simple invitation "Fast and
pray with me this Saturday," as well as the hashtags #Fast4Syria and
#PrayforPeace, thus targeting social media and ease of use through
mobile devices. The photo was made available on September 4 and
went viral on September 5. Through this, in three days the USCCB
was able to reach 572,000 people with information about the day of
prayer by the time it took place on September 7.[24] This example illustrates the potential of social media for official communication in a
way that makes the whole network of people integral to the sharing
of the message. The word about the September 2013 Day of Prayer
and Fasting got out as a joint effort between the USCCB, who officially produced a web site and shareable piece of content, and the
vast network of "unofficial" people who became engaged and passed
it along. Returning to John Paul II's vision for participation and dialogue, in this example we see "the whole Church, strengthened by
each one of its members, more effectively fulfilling its mission for
the life of the world."[25]

24. Information was made available at the United States Conference of Catholic
Bishops Committee on Communications annual meeting, October 9–10, 2013.
25. RD 12, as it quotes *Lumen Gentium* 37.

The concluding thought of *The Rapid Development* is one of inspiration. Bearing the title "To Communicate with the Power of the Spirit," this last section recalls that divine revelation is both the communication of the Word and the illumination of this as truth by the Holy Spirit. In the Spirit, the Word is made discernable, shareable: it moves fully from content to communication as hearers of the Word understand it and are compelled by it to share the Word with others. This work of understanding and sharing is especially animated by the Holy Spirit, as we see in the Pentecost story of Acts 2, where the power of the Spirit fills those gathered in the Upper Room, empowering them with the ability to speak (Acts 2:4). The miracle of languages underscores this, demonstrating how the Spirit moves the communication of the Word even beyond linguistic and cultural barriers.

In highlighting the role of the Spirit, John Paul II urged an "attentive discernment and constant vigilance" vis-à-vis new media, and this too brings to mind the Pentecost moment. The gathering of the disciples in the Upper Room is sometimes interpreted as a time of fear and indecision until the Spirit comes to empower them. While a sense of fear and indecision could be understandable sentiments for a group of people who have just witnessed the death, risen presence, and ascension of their companion and teacher, the first chapter of Acts offers an additional clue. Among the risen Lord's parting words is a promise for the coming of the Holy Spirit, who will come to baptize them, and the command for them to remain in Jerusalem and wait for this gift (Acts 1:4-5). As the disciples gathered on the day of Pentecost, therefore, it is possible that in addition to their sense of fear and indecision, they were prayerfully anticipating the gift of the Spirit in attentive discernment and vigilance. The wisdom therein for media and ministry is prayerful trust in the Spirit who enabled the Church's communication in the first place, and who still comes like a mighty wind to enable us to share the Word in new languages today.

Along these lines, the final words of the document echo the Gospel encouragement that John Paul II made famous: do not be afraid. He urges: do not be afraid of new technologies, of being opposed by the world, and of even one's own weaknesses and inadequacy when it comes to a new medium. We are all learning a new language to tell the Good News, the eternal story that invites us into divine mystery. In our stories, writings, plays, films, broadcasts, and digital interactions, we strive to make present this eternal mystery but cannot in the here and now articulate it fully. At the same time, as John Paul II reminds us, we are called to keep always alive this eternal perspective of heaven and the fullness of hope, grace, and love that was embodied in Jesus Christ (13). As the Spirit gives us the ability to speak this in the language of digital culture, fear, overwhelm, and inadequacy give way to trust in the wisdom of divine revelation and joy in observing Word and Spirit manifest this in new contexts.

World Communications Day Messages

To date, the most recent ecclesial document on social communication is John Paul II's apostolic letter *The Rapid Development*. Since 2005, the annual *World Communications Day Messages* have continued the Church's reflection. They have focused on digital media almost exclusively since 2009. These messages are brief, topical, and emerge out of the process of the Church reading the signs of the times. The brief format of the messages has an important benefit: as they are focused on just one topic, they are released from the responsibility of summing up all the social communication tradition before it, and instead tend to delve deeper into the topic at hand. In recent years, the messages have therefore yielded rich theological reflection and have fueled the ongoing conversation between faith, culture, and the digital age.

The relative brevity of the messages expresses a sign of the times: in a culture where a model blog post is under five hundred words and a tweet is one hundred forty characters or less, a lengthy document challenges the format of information we are becoming accustomed to. With an average length of ten paragraphs each, the *World Communications Day Messages* invite readers quickly, directly, and effectively into the spiritual, pastoral, and ethical realities of digital culture. As we anticipate the next full-length document on social communication, the *World Communications Day Messages* have sustained the conversation. A complete study of these messages is beyond the scope of this chapter but would be a worthwhile topic for further exploration. Here, this chapter closes with a brief overview of the messages as a whole.

The annual celebration of World Communications Day and the accompanying papal message are a recent tradition of the Church initiated by *Inter Mirifica*.[26] Since 1967, there has been an annual message from the pope for this occasion, highlighting a particular aspect of social communication as its annual theme. Paul VI's first message in 1967 echoed the initiatory, constructive, and encouraging themes of *Inter Mirifica* as he underscored the thrust of the conciliar document and foreshadowed the work of *Communio et Progressio*.[27] Over the years, the messages have frequently addressed sociocultural themes concerning international relations, family, youth, women, and the elderly, as well as focusing on particular values such as truth, justice, unity, reconciliation, peace, solidarity, freedom, and progress, and values of key ecclesial relevance such as evangelization. Although generally considering the media as a whole, John Paul II offered a series of messages narrowing the focus to particular ones: computers (1990), video and audiocassettes (1993), television (1994), and cinema (1995). Like John Paul II, Benedict XVI's messages approached a range of sociocultural realities and key values, with a shift after 2009 to acknowledging the media context for each message as particularly digital. Since 2009, these more these more recent "digital messages" of Benedict XVI and now Francis have continued to examine both classic and new topics against this backdrop. This approach is pedagogically significant: rather than viewing the digital media instrumentally, the recent messages have recognized the overall cultural shift wrought by digital communication and thus examine key topics in the context of a broader, digitally shaped culture.

26. *Inter Mirifica* 18.
27. Paul VI, "The Church and Social Communication," First World Communications Day, May 7, 1967, http://www.vatican.va/holy_father/paul_vi/messages/communications/documents/hf_p-vi_mes_19670507_i-com-day_en.html, accessed April 16, 2014.

World Communications Day Messages Addressing the Internet and Digital Media[28]

1990 The Christian Message in a Computer Culture
2001 Preach from the Housetops: The Gospel in the Age of Global Communication
2002 The Internet: A New Forum for Proclaiming the Gospel
2008 The Media: At the Crossroads Between Self-Promotion and Service: Searching for the Truth in Order to Share It with Others
2009 New Technologies, New Relationships: Promoting a Culture of Respect, Dialogue, and Friendship
2010 The Priest and Pastoral Ministry in a Digital World: New Media at the Service of the Word
2011 Truth, Proclamation, and Authenticity of Life in the Digital Age
2012 Silence and Word: Path of Evangelization
2013 Social Networks: Portals of Truth and Faith, New Spaces for Evangelizations
2014 Communication at the Service of an Authentic Culture of Encounter

28. For a complete list of World Communications Day messages since 1967, see http://www.pccs.va/pccs/gmcs/gmcs_eng.htm, accessed April 7, 2014.

6 CHURCH AND SOCIAL COMMUNICATION TODAY

This study invited a dialogue between the Roman Catholic Church's social communication teachings since Vatican II and the challenge of ministerial formation for the digital age. Indispensable for this were the selected documents that provided concrete entry points into the conversation and that rooted us in particular theological, pastoral, and ethical ground for thinking about digital media and ministry. As new teaching documents emerge from the Church, this conversation will continue.

Documents and messages are official forms of ecclesial teaching—a particular teaching medium that conveys the Church's magisterial thought on a topic. Yet teaching is a much broader, multifaceted activity that consists of a plethora of other official and unofficial forms: lectures, presentations, mentoring, modeling, and demonstrating, as well as day-to-day functions, decisions, and relationships that together give form to the professional role of the teacher. The Church's official documents teach, but we can also learn from the broader spectrum of activities that give form to the daily work of the Church as a global institution. For exploring the social communication teachings of the Church for ministry in the digital age, this final chapter turns to this implicit teaching as we examine the work of the Church in social communication today. A departure from previous chapters, which relied on traditional research and analysis of ecclesial documents, this final chapter is the result of in-person observation of the

Church at work, thanks to the hospitality of the Pontifical Council for Social Communication in Rome in the spring of 2014.

The office for the Pontifical Council for Social Communication (PCCS, after the Italian abbreviation) is housed in one of the elegant buildings that line the Via Della Conciliazione, the impressive avenue leading from the Tiber River to St. Peter's Square in Rome. The neighborhood is crowded and busy, full of pilgrims and visitors from all over the world making their way to St. Peter's Square, to the Basilica, or to the Vatican Museums nearby. From the mouths of visitors, tour guides, shopkeepers, waiters, and street vendors, every language is heard. On Sundays and Wednesdays, massive crowds of up to 500,000 people gather in St. Peter's Square, awaiting the appearance of the pope for his Angelus address or weekly General Audience. The pope offers the Angelus address in Italian as the global collection of pilgrims below take in his words—some understanding, some just absorbing the sound. At the Wednesday General Audience, the languages are more formalized: official translations in French, German, English, Spanish, Polish, Portuguese, and Arabic follow the pope's Italian words before all concludes with a common prayer in Latin. Standing in St. Peter's Square amid a global crowd and the sound of many languages, both Babel and Pentecost come to mind: not only the inevitable human confusion in a multilingual crowd of this size but also the sense of unity and even communion in being gathered as Church.

It is compelling to recognize that this is the immediate local context in which the PCCS does its work. When invited to reflect on this, Archbishop Claudio Maria Celli, the president of the PCCS, offered a profound image: the architecture of St. Peter's Square itself as inspiration for the mission and vision of his office.[1] As Archbishop Celli recounts, when in the mid-seventeenth century, Bernini showed Pope Alexander VII his plans for the piazza in front of the new St. Peter's Basilica, the pope made a special request for an elliptical space, with the right and left colonnades embracing the piazza as if they were giant arms extending from the basilica to embrace the pilgrims approaching it. Crowning these arms, a statue of Christ stands at the top center of the basilica's façade, flanked by the apostles. From this

---

1. Claudio Maria Celli, personal interview, February 20, 2014.

central group the saints extend out: on the top of the left and right colonnades are statues of saints in a regular row, a cloud of witnesses in stone surrounding the square. The architecture of their solid white forms brings a heavenly stillness over the hustle and bustle of the global crowd below, both grounding and elevating the experience of the people in the square toward a greater mystery. For Archbishop Celli, Bernini's colonnade is an evocative symbol of the mission and vision of his work, helping to facilitate the Church's communication toward authentic community and communion.

While the façade, statues, and colonnades are essential to the architecture of St. Peter's Square, they in themselves are incomplete without the people who fill the square. The regular row of saints communicates together with the irregular ebb and flow of people below them, packed in as a crowd or meandering in every direction, in groups or alone, representing the imperfect and irregular human condition in their sheer diversity in this transcendent architectural setting. In the square, the triumphant Christ and the cloud of witnesses embrace the multilingual, multicultural, multifaceted crowd below, communicating unity and a shared sacramentality of place and inviting them into communion as they approach the basilica. As Celli notes, the beauty of St. Peter's Square communicates the grace of communion: even if one enters the space alone, the architectural symbols receive and embrace the pilgrim, as do the symbols of Christ and the saints expressing a profound accompaniment with those walking the streets of the world today.[2] In the digital age, when our experiences of pastoral ministry can seem as frenetic, multilingual, and multidirectional as the bustling crowds through St. Peter's Square, Christ and the cloud of witnesses that embrace our experience and invite us into heavenly communion convey stability through our common rootedness in the Gospel, and in the age-old task to proclaim it. Along with the words "do not be afraid" cited in this book's introduction, St. Peter's Square offers another profoundly encouraging metaphor for thinking about ministry in our digital context. When overwhelmed by the challenge of this cultural shift, Christ and the cloud of witnesses remind us that we are surrounded and embraced by heavenly witnesses to the proclamation of the Word, communicators of Good

2. Ibid.

News now in triumph. As we struggle to listen and to announce, to encounter and to be present in the digital age, we are reminded of our communion with this heavenly reality, a vision to shape our communication here and now.

As the square's cloud of witnesses conveys, communication of the Gospel is not a singular effort. Likewise, various aspects of social communication at the Vatican fall on multiple offices, among these Vatican Radio and Television, the internet office overseeing vatican .va, the Vatican newspaper *L'Osservatore Romano*, the *Sala Stampa* or Press Office of the Holy See, the *Libreria Editirice Vaticana* (the Vatican Publishing House), the Pontifical Council for Social Communications overseeing news.va and pccs.va, and the Secretariat of State, which all work on some aspect of social communication. At first glance this large number of offices that "officially communicate" could pose a bureaucratic challenge, especially in our culture of fast-flowing information that demands the latest and definitive word; when there are this many sources, not counting the pope himself, quick and cohesive communication can be a challenge. With the increasing availability of digital communication to all, Pope Francis himself can choose to communicate through none of these means and instead stand with young people for a "selfie" or share his words through an iPhone video recording, as he did to Kenneth Copeland Ministries in February of 2014.[3] At the same time, it is evident that at the Vatican, official communication is embedded in a collaborative network of these offices, which is perhaps more true to the reality of digital culture than just one single source. In the coexistence and collaboration of these offices, Vatican social communication is a network. In some measure, it experiences internally the gifts and challenges of the networked communication of our greater digital culture.

Embedded in this institutional communication network, the PCCS serves to reflect on and engage practically in social communication for the Church. They call the greater Church to think broadly about social communication, not as a side activity of ministry but as some-

3. In February 2014, Pope Francis shared a video message with a gathering of Kenneth Copeland Ministries via the iPhone of personal friend Bishop Tony Palmer. Full recording available at http://www.youtube.com/watch?v=b5TwrG8B3ME, accessed May 2, 2014.

thing integral to the very identity and mission of the Church. In their work to serve the Church both in Rome and globally, the PCCS strives to illuminate the cultural shift that has emerged in and through digital communication. This shift reveals that social communication now is beyond an instrumental understanding of incorporating the use of media into one's ministry. Rather, social communication in the digital age understands itself as embedded in the total cultural context that has been shaped by the reality of digital communication, a culture where the distinction between online and offline is becoming less helpful, as the experience of digital communication has wrought comprehensive changes in how we understand and relate to one another and how we go about gaining knowledge and understanding. As Archbishop Celli sums it up, the PCCS aims to help the Church as a whole to perceive that the actual technologies are creating a cultural milieu where we are living and where we are called to announce the Gospel.[4]

Language and Traditions of Digital Culture

There are millions of people who visit the Vatican each year, many of them coming from foreign lands. They experience Italy as a country with a foreign language and new cultural traditions. Anyone who has traveled abroad has experienced this: the simultaneous strangeness and familiarity of context, the brain's effort to make sense of a language and culture while immersed in it, an experience that is qualitatively different from learning phrases and conjugations in a language course or reading a tourist's guidebook. If digital media are giving form to a new cultural milieu, then understanding the digital media demands a cultural lens: one that considers the language and the traditions of this new context. Instrumentality in the digital age only goes as far as the language course or guidebook when visiting a foreign land; to fully understand the new context, one has to approach it as a full immersion of one's reality into this culture. Along these lines, Monsignor Paul Tighe, secretary of the PCCS, urges special attention to language—its form, mode, and content—when it comes

4. Ibid.

to social communication in the digital age.[5] Engaging in social communication through the most innovative platform is a great start, but without awareness of the particular form, mode, and content intelligible in the digital age, this could lead to a frustrating experience. In addition to offering new platforms for communication, digital culture is also shaping communication into an interactive, conversational, and playful form, an increasingly visual and multimedia mode, and demands content that is able to express the tradition through the vocabulary, symbols, and metaphors that make sense today. Awareness of the form, mode, and content of communication is as essential to respecting the culture of digital communication as finding the most relevant platform to participate in so as to reach people today with the Good News.

Along with this attention to language, Msgr. Tighe also names some cultural traditions found within the digital context, what he calls "key drivers in a digital culture": friendship, searching, sharing, and following.[6] These four drivers are everyday ways of digital communication, discernable in our engagement with social networking in the way we connect with people in and around information. Yet they are also indicators of potential for deeper meaning in the digital realm. From the perspective of the Church's mission to proclaim the Gospel, these four drivers are entry points into a cultural dialogue toward such deeper meaning. Friendship as emerging from the act of "friending" and connecting with people in a network is an entry point that leads more deeply into true relationality *in imago Trinitatis*. Searching—fundamental to our browsing, researching, and gathering of information online—raises the deeper question of the desire for truth and our ongoing quest for it. Sharing, as we pass along the information we find or content we create, calls to mind the authentic gift of self and the integral standards of persons-in-communion when it comes to the communication of content. Finally, following as we commit ourselves to the digital presence of others invites the deeper themes of hospitality to the other, receptivity, dialogue, and even discipleship. Keeping these four drivers of digital culture in mind as some of this new culture's "traditions" shapes ministry in the digital

---

5. Paul Tighe, personal interview, February 18, 2014.
6. Ibid.

context with a cultural sensitivity that extends hospitality to people's fundamental questions and dialogues so as to offer an invitation to the deeper truth of the Gospel.

Based on this comprehensive cultural approach to social communication in the digital age, the PCCS continues to serve the Church in specific ways: running formation programs for bishops and seminaries around the world, inviting dialogue regarding social communication from the academy, publishing teaching documents, and serving the pope in his engagement with the World Communications Day themes and messages each year. There are also a number of concrete ways the PCCS engages in social communication, demonstrating through these its practical understanding of digital media and ministry: collaborating with the Secretariat of State on the papal Twitter account, hosting a digital global network of Catholic communicators through intermirifica.net, aggregating Vatican news on news.va and its related "Pope App" as an accessible one-stop digital portal, and maintaining an interactive social media presence through platforms like Facebook, Twitter, and Pinterest. Experimenting with interactivity through social media raises a number of intriguing questions for the PCCS, shedding new light on the challenge of an official, institutional presence in a digital context of interactivity, collaboration, and playfulness.

In its activity on social media like Twitter and Facebook, the PCCS is an official institution in a playful, collaborative, unofficial context. This is a gift and a challenge; according to Msgr. Tighe, for an institutional figure on social media, playfulness is more ambiguous, as not everyone will understand playfulness the same way, and ultimately the institution is responsible for what they reasonably foresee as something people might misunderstand.[7] As the Vatican brings to mind for many not playfulness but rather tradition, formality, and reverence, it might be shocking or even offensive for some to convey a social media presence straying too far from this perception. At the same time, the approachability and the down-to-earth demeanor of Pope Francis has captured the world's attention, his accessibility to people documented in a growing number of stories and images. In late January of 2014, graffiti of Pope Francis depicted as a superhero

7. Ibid.

appeared on a wall near the Vatican, and the PCCS captured the image and shared it through its Twitter feed, with the comment: "We share with you a graffiti found on a Roman street near the Vatican." With 2800 re-tweets and 1200 "likes," this playful image became the PCCS's most interactive tweet, signaling a unique alignment between the nature of the medium and the content of the message, and evoking a great response from people to an image that juxtaposes the formal and the informal. While the photo itself brings a smile to most people, the fact that the PCCS tweeted it figured as an important part of the story as the global media reported on it. *The Daily Mail* titled its story on the graffiti as "Let Us Spray: Graffiti Depicting the Pope as a Superhero Gets Official Approval from the Vatican, Who Tweet It to Their 84,000 Followers," and the story by the National Public Radio (NPR) likewise noted that "the Vatican communications department showed its approval."[8] The playful image clearly resonating with the nature of social media intrigued many, not only for its content but also for its origin as shared "from the Vatican."

As an institution, the Church continues to grapple with its formal image in less formal contexts and circumstances. This is an important question on the diocesan and parish level as well. Ministry as an activity of the Church always carries an official connotation, and pastoral leaders are representing the Good News of Jesus Christ as well as the institution tasked to communicate it in word and deed. In the informal, playful atmosphere of the social network, it remains an opportunity and a challenge to explore the meaning of "official" presence.

In practice, Pope Francis himself is exploring this question, and his is an additional example of the Church's social communication practices in the digital age. The Vatican's social communication network of radio, television, internet, press, and social media regularly

---

8. Jill Reilly, "Let Us Spray: Graffiti Depicting Pope as a Superhero gets Official Approval from the Vatican who Tweet it to their 84,000 Followers," *The Daily Mail*, January 29, 2014, http://www.dailymail.co.uk/news/article-2547919/Let -spray-Graffiti-depicting-Pope-superhero-gets-official-approval-Vatican-tweet -84-000-followers.html, accessed April 7, 2014; Sylvia Poggioli, "On A Roman Street Graffiti Celebrates 'Superpope,'" Parallels NPR Blog, January 29, 2014, http:// www.npr.org/blogs/parallels/2014/01/29/268361194/on-a-roman-street -graffiti-celebrates-superpope, accessed April 7, 2014.

convey the presence of the pontiff in textual and audiovisual form. Through both his personal witness and his theological reflection on communication, encounter has been key to understanding how Pope Francis envisions being present to the people he serves. In his 2014 World Communications Day message, "Communication at the Service of an Authentic Culture of Encounter," Pope Francis reflected on the parable of the Good Samaritan as a parable for communication. He emphasized: "It is not enough to be passersby on the digital highways, simply "connected"; connections need to grow into true encounters. We cannot live apart, closed in on ourselves. We need to love and to be loved. We need tenderness."[9] Openness to others, gestures and expressions of love, and tenderness animate Pope Francis's public presence, whether he is washing inmates' feet, embracing the afflicted, sharing the stage with the least important among us, or sharing his birthday breakfast with the homeless and their dogs. Each of these examples is a powerful image that exemplifies his face-to-face encounters and what it is that has captured the world about his personality and leadership. As Msgr. Tighe reflects, this is an important lesson for social communication in the digital age: the gestures and encounters of Pope Francis are media that powerfully communicate the message of the Gospel before words.[10] As our communication options expand, how compelling the genuine human encounter is will remain an important parameter for pastoral ministry and communication.

Pope Francis's formal engagement with the media has also reflected this openness to encounter: although not the first pope to offer an interview, his personal availability and openness to the press has been new.[11] His in-depth interview in the fall of 2013 with Fr. Antonio Spadaro, SJ, revealed his personal side, as did his gesture of calling Eugenio Scalfari, the founder of the Italian paper *La Repubblica* to

9. Francis, "Communication at the Service of an Authentic Culture of Encounter," Forty-Eighth World Communications Day Message, January 24, 2014. http://www.vatican.va/holy_father/francesco/messages/communications /documents/papa-francesco_20140124_messaggio-comunicazioni-sociali _en.html, accessed April 7, 2014.

10. Paul Tighe, personal interview, February 18, 2014.

11. John Paul II offered two interviews to Polish journalist Jas Gawronski in 1988 and 1993, and in 2005 Benedict XVI granted an interview to Polish television.

accept and arrange for an interview.[12] Approaching the media with openness and availability, Pope Francis is recognizing and honoring the potential of social communication as a path to genuine encounter. As noted above, in February of 2014, Pope Francis reinforced this with something genuinely new: a personal video message captured on an iPhone. While receiving a visit from Bishop Tony Palmer, a Protestant leader and personal friend, he offered a brief greeting and message on unity to a group of Pentecostal Americans gathered for a conference that Palmer was participating in.[13] Palmer captured the message on his iPhone, shared it as part of the conference, and it gained global attention as a result. Remarkable here is the pope's immediacy, his sense of real, intimate presence that the video conveys; a departure from his formal appearances, even by his down-to-earth, approachable standard. Viewing the video feels like sitting across from the pope in conversation as he shares impromptu but profound wisdom. The immediacy of the iPhone camera conveys an experience in many ways more intimate than seeing Pope Francis in person in the crowd of 500,000 at St. Peter's Square. Although a mediated presence, in the iPhone message Pope Francis recognizes the potential for inviting genuine encounter and shares of himself in this unprecedented way, creating an unofficial public communication of the most official public office in the Church. For digital media and ministry, this play between official and unofficial echoes the challenge of the graffiti above. It also demonstrates the sheer power of genuine encounter and its value as an ultimate standard for pastoral communication.

The question of presence infuses social communication for the Church in the digital age. Archbishop Celli perceives the challenge of changing technologies not as a race to keep up with the latest gadget, but rather as a continued exploration of how the Church is present in the milieu created by new technologies and how by its presence

12. Antonio Spadaro, "A Big Heart Open to God," as published by *America*, September 30, 2013, http://www.americamagazine.org/pope-interview, accessed April 7, 2014; Eugenio Scalfari, "Pope: How the Church will Change," *La Repubblica*, October 1, 2013, http://www.repubblica.it/cultura/2013/10/01/news /pope_s_conversation_with_scalfari_english-67643118/, accessed April 7, 2014.

13. See Francis's iPhone message on Christian unity at: http://www.youtube .com/watch?v=TsEJVP_eDAE, accessed April 7, 2014.

the Church announces the Gospel therein.[14] Thinking about how the Church is present raises the fundamental question of what is meant by Church. Understanding the digital culture as a networked and collaborative reality, Msgr. Tighe envisions the Church's presence as a "devolved interactivity" that broadens the understanding of the Church from just the pope, magisterium, and curial offices to a global network of the people of God.[15] Articulating a perspective of practical subsidiarity, he notes that for the Church to engage in dialogue with people's questions and search for meaning, it does not have to be the pope commenting on every blog, feed, profile, and web site. As all who are baptized share in the Church's fundamental evangelizing mission to communicate the Good News, all who belong to the Church share the responsibility to communicate the Church's presence in the digital milieu. Saint Paul's image of the Body of Christ offers relevant meaning here, as many parts within the body function together to make present Christ in the world. Likewise, @Pontifex not only inspires but also functions together with the youth group's social media page, the Catholic thinker's blog, the Facebook activity of a person who self-identifies as Roman Catholic on his or her profile, the web site of a religious community, and the YouTube channel of a service organization to convey "Church" in the digital milieu. Together, the web of these different groups presents a complex image. As in 1 Corinthians, the many parts are unified in one body. The digital presence of the Church likewise needs a unifying foundation, an element that moves these parts from interconnectedness toward an expression of communion. As bustling pilgrims in St. Peter's Square, we are learning what this means in the digital culture of our time.

14. Claudio Maria Celli, personal interview, February 20, 2014.
15. Paul Tighe, personal interview, February 18, 2014.

EPILOGUE

Each day at noon, the people working in the offices of the PCCS pause their work and gather for prayer. They join in prayer with the age-old tradition of the Church to recite the Angelus, a prayer that marvels at the mystery of the incarnation, the Word becoming flesh and dwelling among us.

℣. The angel of the Lord declared unto Mary,
℟. And she conceived of the Holy Spirit.

Hail Mary, full of grace, the Lord is with thee. Blessed art thou amongst women, and blessed is the fruit of thy womb, Jesus. Holy Mary, Mother of God, pray for us sinners, now and at the hour of our death. Amen.

℣. Behold the handmaid of the Lord.
℟. Be it done unto me according to thy Word.

Hail Mary . . .

℣. And the Word was made flesh.
℟. And dwelt amongst us.

Hail Mary . . .

℣. Pray for us, O Holy Mother of God.
℟. That we may be made worthy of the promises of Christ.

Let us pray: Pour forth, we beseech thee, O Lord, your grace into our hearts, that we to whom the incarnation of Christ Thy Son was made known by the message of an angel, may by His Passion and Cross be brought to the glory of His resurrection; through the same Christ our Lord.

R℣. Amen.

Mary's openness to the Word transformed her, so that through her the Word could be born as Christ, dwell among us, and proclaim the invitation and promise of salvation. The prayer is one of engagement, openness, transforming encounter, real presence, and Good News. For social communication and the Church, this prayer encapsulates the foundation and the hope for proclaiming Christ today.

In our digital age, our words can connect us or cut us deeply. They can be words of self-promotion or of self-gift. They can mock or heal, play or ponder, edify or confuse, celebrate or lament our human experience. In this context, the Church's task to proclaim Good News is infused with a new mission to offer human communication the hope of the Word Incarnate, a hope that moves human connection toward the image of human-divine communion. Proclaiming Christ today necessarily involves the culture wrought by digital communication; our question is no longer if, but how.

BIBLIOGRAPHY

Albertigo, Giuseppe, and Joseph A. Komonchak. *History of Vatican II: The Formation of the Council's Identity, First Period and Intersession, October 1962–September 1963*. Vol. 2. Maryknoll, NY: Orbis Books, 1997.

Benedict XVI. "Message for the 46th World Day of Communications: Silence and Word: Path to Evangelization," January 24, 2012. http://www.vatican.va/holy_father/benedict_xvi/messages /communications/documents/hf_ben-xvi_mes_20120124 _46th-world-communications-day_en.html.

———. "Message for the 47th World Day of Communications: Social Networks: Portals of Truth and Faith; New Spaces for Evangelization." January 24, 2013. http://www.vatican.va/holy_father /benedict_xvi/messages/communications/documents/hf _ben-xvi_mes_20130124_47th-world-communications-day _en.html.

———. "Message for the 43rd World Day of Communications: New Technologies, New Relationships: Promoting a Culture of Respect, Dialogue, and Friendship." January 24, 2009. http:// www.vatican.va/holy_father/benedict_xvi/messages/com munications/documents/hf_ben-xvi_mes_20090124_43rd -world-communications-day_en.html.

Bray, Peter. "When Is My Tweet's Prime of Life? (A Brief Statistical Interlude)." The MOZ Blog, November 12, 2012. http://moz .com/blog/when-is-my-tweets-prime-of-life.

Bunson, Matthew E. "The History and Development of Post-Conciliar Catholic Social Communications." In *Foundation Theology 2007: Student Essays for Ministry Professionals*, 205–27. South Bend, IN: Cloverdale, 2007.

Campbell, Heidi. "Understanding the Relationship between Religion Online and Offline in a Networked Society." *Journal of the American Academy of Religion* 80, no. 1 (March 2012): 64–93.

Celli, Claudio Maria. "Social Communication." *AFER* 51, no. 3 (2009): 185–92.

———. Personal Interview, February 20, 2014.

Cheong, Pauline Hope. "Authority." In *Digital Religion: Understanding Religious Practices in New Media Worlds*. Edited by Heidi Campbell. New York: Routledge, 2013.

Coleman, John, and Miklos Tomka. Mass Media. Vol. 6. *Concilium*. Norwich: SCM Press, 1993.

Congregation for Catholic Education. "Guide to the Training of Future Priests Concerning the Instruments of Social Communication," 1986. http://www.vatican.va/roman_curia /pontifical_councils/pccs/documents/rc_pc_pccs_doc _19031986_guide-for-future-priests_en.html.

Council Daybook: Vatican II Session 1 (October 11 to December 8, 1962) and Session 2 (September 29 to December 4, 1963). Washington DC: National Catholic Welfare Conference, 1965.

Cousineau, Jacques. "L'Eglise et Mass Media." Les Cahiers D'etudes et Des Recherches 16 (1973). http://www.officecom.qc.ca /indexSiteOCS/Documentation/Cahiers/Cahier16.pdf.

Deskur, Andrzej. "Twentieth Anniversary of *Communio et Progressio*: Post-Conciliar Instruction Seen as Last Council Document." *Osservatore Romano* (English) 1180 (1991): 2.

Drescher, Elizabeth, and Anderson, Keith. *Click 2 Save: The Digital Ministry Bible*. New York: Morehouse, 2012.

Dulles, Avery Robert. *The Craft of Theology*. New York: Crossroad, 1992.

———. "Vatican II and Communications." In V*atican II Assessment and Perspectives Twenty-Five Years After (1962–1987)*. Edited by Rene Latourelle. 3:528–47. Mahwah, NJ: Paulist Press, 1989.

Eilers, Franz-Josef. *Communicating Church: Social Communication Documents*. Manila, Philippines: Logos, 2011.

————. *Communicating in Ministry and Mission*. Vol. Third. Manila, Philippines: Logos, 2009.

————. "The Communication Formation of Church Leaders as a Holistic Concern." In *Mediating Religion: Conversations in Media, Religion and Culture*. Edited by Jolyon Mitchell and Sophia Marriage. London: T & T Clark, 2003.

Faniran, J. O. "*Aetatis Novae*: Pastoral Instruction on Social Communication on the 20th Anniversary of *Communio et Progressio*." *AFER* 34, no. 6 (1992): 364–75.

Francis. "Message for the 48th World Day of Communications: Communication at the Service of an Authentic Culture of Encounter," January 24, 2014. http://www.vatican.va/holy_father /francesco/messages/communications/documents/papa -francesco_20140124_messaggio-comunicazioni-sociali_en.html.

Gould, Meredith. *Social Media Gospel*. Collegeville, MN: Liturgical Press, 2013.

Haring, Bernard. "Ethics of Communication." In *Free and Faithful in Christ*, 153–99. New York: Seabury Press, 1979.

Heidegger, Martin. "On The Question Concerning Technology." In *Basic Writings*, 307–42. San Francisco: HarperSanFrancisco, 1993.

Jenkins, Henry, Ravi Purushotma, Margaret Weigel, Katie Clinton, and Alice J. Robinson. *Confronting the Challenges of Participatory Culture*. Cambridge, MA: MIT Press, 2009. http:// mitpress.mit.edu/sites/default/files/titles/free_download /9780262513623_Confronting_the_Challenges.pdf.

John Paul II. *Catechesi Tradendae*. 1979. http://www.vatican.va /holy_father/john_paul_ii/apost_exhortations/documents /hf_jp-ii_exh_16101979_catechesi-tradendae_en.html.

————. *Pastores Dabo Vobis*. 1992. http://www.vatican.va/holy_father /john_paul_ii/apost_exhortations/documents/hf_jp-ii_exh _25031992_pastores-dabo-vobis_en.html.

————. "The Rapid Development," 2005. http://www.vatican.va /holy_father/john_paul_ii/apost_letters/documents/hf_jp-ii _apl_20050124_il-rapido-sviluppo_en.html.

Kampe, Walther. "Communicating with the World: The Decree Inter Mirifica." In *Vatican II Revisited by Those Who Were There*, 195–201. London: Geoffrey Chapman, 1986.

Lamberigts, Mathijs. "The Discussion of the Modern Media." In *History of Vatican II*. Edited by Joseph A. Komonchak and Giuseppe Alberigo, II: 267–79. Maryknoll, NY: Orbis Books, 1997.

Latourelle, Rene. *Theology of Revelation: Including Commentary on the Constitution Dei Verbum of Vatican II*. San Francisco: Wipf and Stock, 2009.

Lewis, C. S. *The Great Divorce*. San Francisco: Harper Collins Edition, 2001.

Lytle, Julie. *Faith Formation 4.0: Introducing an Ecology of Faith in a Digital Age*. New York: Morehouse, 2013.

Martin, Allan, and Jan Grudziecki. "DigEuLit: Concepts and Tools for Digital Literacy Development." *Innovation in Teaching and Learning in Information and Computer Sciences* (ITALICS) 5, no. 4 (2006): 249–67.

Overend, Paul. "Education or Formation? The Issue of Personhood in Learning for Ministry." *Journal of Adult Theological Education* 4, no. 2 (2007): 133–48. doi:10.1558/jate2007v4i2.133.

Paul VI. "Evangelii Nuntiandi" (Evangelization in the Modern World). Vatican web site. http://www.vatican.va/holy_father/paul_vi/apost_exhortations/documents/hf_p-vi_exh_19751208_evangelii-nuntiandi_en.html.

Pontifical Council for Social Communication. "Communio et Progressio" (On the Means of Social Communication). Vatican web site. http://www.vatican.va/roman_curia/pontifical_councils/pccs/documents/rc_pc_pccs_doc_23051971_communio_en.html.

———. "Aetatis Novae" (On Social Communications on the Twentieth Anniversary of *Communio et Progressio*). Vatican web site. http://www.vatican.va/roman_curia/pontifical_councils/pccs/documents/rc_pc_pccs_doc_22021992_aetatis_en.html.

———. *The Church and Internet*. Vatican web site. http://www.vatican.va/roman_curia/pontifical_councils/pccs/documents/rc_pc_pccs_doc_20020228_church-internet_en.html.

———. *Ethics in Internet*. Vatican web site. http://www.vatican.va/roman_curia/pontifical_councils/pccs/documents/rc_pc_pccs_doc_20020228_ethics-internet_en.html.

Ruszkowski, Andre. "The Decree on the Means of Social Communication: Success or Failure of the Council?" In *Vatican II Assessment and Perspectives Twenty-Five Years After (1962–1987)*. Edited by Rene Latourelle, 548–79. Mahwah, NJ: Paulist Press, 1989.

Rynne, Xavier. *Letters from Vatican City: Vatican Council II (First Session): Background and Debates*. New York: Farrar, Strauss, and Company, 1963.

Schmidthus, Karlheinz. "Decree on the Instruments of Social Communication." In *Commentary on the Documents of Vatican II*. Edited by Herbert Vorgrimler, 1:89–104. New York: Herder and Herder, 1967.

Second Vatican Council. *Sacrosanctum Concilium* (Constitution on the Sacred Liturgy). Vatican web site. http://www.vatican.va/archive/hist_councils/ii_vatican_council/documents/vat-ii_const_19631204_sacrosanctum-concilium_en.html.

———. *Inter Mirifica* (Decree on the Mass Media). Vatican web site. http://www.vatican.va/archive/hist_councils/ii_vatican_council/documents/vat-ii_decree_19631204_inter-mirifica_en.html.

———. *Lumen Gentium* (Dogmatic Constitution on the Church). Vatican web site. http://www.vatican.va/archive/hist_councils/ii_vatican_council/documents/vat-ii_const_19641121_lumen-gentium_en.html.

———. *Dei Verbum* (Dogmatic Constitution on Divine Revelation). Vatican web site. http://www.vatican.va/archive/hist_councils/ii_vatican_council/documents/vat-ii_const_19651118_dei-verbum_en.html.

———. *Gaudium et Spes* (Pastoral Constitution on Church in the Modern World). Vatican web site. http://www.vatican.va/archive/hist_councils/ii_vatican_council/documents/vat-ii_cons_19651207_gaudium-et-spes_en.html.

———. *Optatam Totius* (Decree on Priestly Training). Vatican web site. http://www.vatican.va/archive/hist_councils/ii_vatican_council/documents/vat-ii_decree_19651028_optatam-totius_en.html.

Selwyn, Neil Selwyn, "Reconsidering Political Popular Understandings of the Digital Divide," *New Media & Society* 6, no. 3 (2004): 344–45.

Shirky, Clay. *Cognitive Surplus: Creativity and Generosity in a Connected Age*. New York: Penguin Press, 2010.

Soukup, Paul A. *Christian Communication: A Bibliographical Survey.* Vol. 14. Bibliographies and Indexes in Religious Studies. New York: Greenwood Press, 1989.

———. "Church Documents and the Media." In *Mass Media*. Edited by John Coleman and Miklos Tomka, 6:71–79. London: SCM Press, 1993.

Sullivan, Maureen. *101 Questions & Answers on Vatican II.* Mahwah, NJ: Paulist Press, 2002.

Tanner, Norman. *The Church and the World: Gaudium et Spes, Inter Mirifica.* Rediscovering Vatican II. Mahwah, NJ: Paulist Press, 2005.

Tighe, Paul. Personal Interview, February 18, 2014.

Turkle, Sherry. *Alone Together: Why We Expect More from Technology and Less from Each Other.* New York: Basic Books, 2011.

Vogt, Brandon. *The Church and New Media.* Huntington, IN: Our Sunday Visitor, 2011.

White, Robert. "Mass Media and Culture in Contemporary Catholicism: The Significance of Vatican II." In *Vatican II Assessment and Perspectives Twenty-Five Years After (1962–1987).* Edited by Rene Latourelle, 580–611. Mahwah, NJ: Paulist Press, 1989.

Zickuhr, Kathryn and Aaron Smith. "Digital Differences." Pew Internet & American Life Project, April 13, 2012, 1–2. http://www.pewinternet.org/Reports/2012/Digital-differences.aspx.

Zickuhr Kathryn. "Who's Not Online and Why," Pew Internet and American Life Project. September 25, 2013. http://pewinternet.org/Reports/2013/Non-internet-users.aspx.

Zsupan-Jerome, Daniella. "Creative Communication: Digital Creativity and Theology in Dialogue." *New Theology Review* 26, no. 2 (April 2014): 80–87.

INDEX